DOWN IN THE VALLEY

DOWN IN THE VALLEY

MICHAEL SNEDEKER

CLEAR
GLASS
PUBLICATIONS

San Francisco • Portland, Oregon

ACKNOWLEDGMENTS

Many thanks to the Bilingual Press/Editorial Bilingüe of Arizona State University in Tempe, Arizona, for granting permission to reprint Poem 12 from *Poems of the Aztec Peoples* (1983), translated by Edward Kissam and Michael Schmidt.

FIRST EDITION

ISBN 0-931-425-23-9

Cover design and illustration by Vicki Trego Hill
Typeset by Anna Taylor
Printed on acid-free paper by McNaughton & Gunn, Inc.,
of Saline, Michigan.

∞

To Frederick Beckett Snedeker-Short

The butterfly
sipping:
the flower
my open heart,
friends,
a fragrant flower.

Now I scatter it
as rain.

Nezahualcoyotl

DOWN IN THE VALLEY

Prologue
—July 3, 1976

Sergio Magon walked down the long spinal corridor, nodding, joking, jiving his way through a half mile of dense morning traffic until he came to the steel door of the Fly's wing. He opened the door and entered. Two bulbs caged in wire mesh glared in pools on the slick concrete floor but barely penetrated the rows of cells on either side. The old man's cell was near the wing's end on the left, the twenty-ninth of thirty-two cells. It was a model of organization, a room smaller than a ping-pong table jammed to the ceiling with clippings, files, boxes and books so ordered that the old man could lay his hands on the materials he wanted without missing a single beat of his verbal riffs, or somehow (when he was in a mood to show off) without taking his eyes off whomever he was addressing. Legal wizardry by the Fly had paved the way for Sergio's t-shirt announcing his Union membership that he was allowed to wear only after the springy old fellow had plastered copies of a court victory on the t-shirt question all over the central corridor. Sergio anticipated stepping out this morning with a radical break from his normal behavior. He would open their game with his queen bishop's pawn instead of the inevitable P-K4.

No one was in the hall except a young White dude he had not seen before and a Mexican from Texas. They were down at the other end, backlit by the fluorescence of the staff office across from the old man's cell. Most residents of the wing had gone to work or back to sleep after morning count.

The two others in the hall were walking toward him and the door behind.

He stayed to the right. The White moved over to the opposite row of cells, but the Mexican stayed on Sergio's side walking straight toward him. Hair prickled slightly on the back of Sergio's neck, and settled down when the Mexican moved from the right to the middle where he belonged.

The heavy door opened and clanged shut behind. Sergio exchanged nods with the White, and nodded to the Mexican. The Mexican looked him in the eye, nodded once, and then lunged for and locked onto his right arm. He lifted and closed his right hand, catching the Mexican's face with his fist, but did not shake the Mexican from his arm. He lifted his left hand to strike, but the White gripped his wrist with both hands. He kicked at kneecaps and shins. Amidst the grunts and gasps he heard the squeak of tennis shoes flying towards him from the rear, and he surged and twisted with new force.

The sluggish, heavy air opened. He saw the Mexican's groin turn toward him, and struck it with his knee as easily as he could spear a cooked carrot with a fork. The Mexican doubled over, but did not release the clamphold on his arm. They were pulling him down. He stepped forward to regain his footing and yanked himself up, just in time to feel a numb shock course through his body and hear the soft rip of a knife entering his lower back. "Help!" he cried reflexively, more out of duty or irresistible friction than hope.

"Guard! Anderson! Get your fat ass into the hall! Someone's gettin' hurt!" It was the Fly's voice from down the hall. Other prisoners watched silently from the shadows in back of their cells, their eyes glowing in the dark. The only other sound he heard was the rumbling tear of his own flesh.

"Magon!" A voice boomed behind him and rang through the wing. He turned and saw, over a pockmarked neck, his friend Fred Johnson running toward him. His eyes locked on Fred: blue denimed knees lifting high, pumping black arms corded with veins and muscles, fine beads of sweat materializing all over his bald head, a flattish nose splayed across his face, a face normally mobile and expressive that was now the only thing about Fred that was still.

The air hummed as he fell, his eyes locked on Fred. Thank God I'm falling so slowly, he thought, Fred can catch me before I drop. But Fred's legs were slower, they seemed to be pushing through thick syrup. It was a free fall down without gravity's normal toll, and although Fred was not going to be able to catch him, he was glad that Fred was coming, glad that he was given Fred's body straining toward him as a final place to rest his eyes.

I

The Fly's Journal
—undated

I WANT TO TALK ABOUT DOING TIME. DOING TIME IS AN ACTIVE concept. Time is done by people who do not want to be done by time, that is, rotated slowly over a simmering fire for ten years and finally delivered to be eaten by the streets.

How can time be done? In all the ordinary ways: taking care of business, academic study, kissing ass, playing handball, dominoes or chess, etc., and in extraordinary ways. Like the rich, we prisoners have an abundance of time on our hands. Unlike the rich, we are not cursed with obligatory distractions, are not expected by anyone to become the connoisseurs of consumption that the wealthy dedicate themselves to becoming. No one here can now name the best restaurants in San Francisco or New York. No one is expected to distinguish several levels of wine quality or know about the nuances of changing fashion in clothing, accessories, automobiles, or vacation spots. Though limited in our spatial movements, we have more time than either the poor, who must trade their time and labor for the wherewithal to maintain themselves, or the rich, who are expected to behave in such a manner that they are commonly heard to complain about their lack of time "for themselves."

Prisoners have so much time that they must come directly to terms with its abundance as well as the severe constraint on Time's sister, Space. A widely followed principle in prison is, Never tell a story in two minutes when it can be stretched to ten. Another: Every opportunity to elongate a transaction should be seized.

The pathology of time: every transaction with the outside world is worried over, toyed with, analyzed, inflated, stepped on, relived in other contexts, and generally wrung for much, much more than it is worth.

This is an example of being done by time; prisoners are often led by incessant ruminations over a visit that was but one of many incidents in the more varied life of one "outside," to views that strike the outsider as bizarre, even paranoid. Grave misunderstandings result from a simple misallocation of meaning. A letter hastily written by an attorney, the fourth in a series of twelve, or by a relative hurrying to finish before preparing supper for hungry children, is parsed here with all the hermeneutic zeal of a Kabbalist attacking the Pentateuch.

A person with no resources other than time can explore the mind more thoroughly than one who has access to all of space and matter as well. The superabundance offered by prison permits researches that no one else has time to do.

My mental ventures outside prison walls began when I was locked in the Hole years ago for filing an annoying lawsuit. I lay still on my steel bed, and after a time I floated up to the top of my room. I bounced gently off the ceiling, and turned to see my body laid out on the bed beneath, calm and ready for burial. It was very intense.

Soon, I was moving through the prison corridors, even into plush official offices. For quite a while I was more interested in exploring the prison than leaving, but eventually I flew over the walls and all around the North American continent, at whatever speed or height I wished. I had made five or six such trips before my last one, a trip taken at night.

I visited the Midwestern library where I committed the first of the thefts that brought me to the attention of the authorities. A handful of students were studying late in the evening. It was quiet, peaceful. I finally turned away and tried to come back here, but I got lost! I panicked, and flew with ever-increasing speed until everything beneath me blurred. I could not find California, let alone the Central Valley or the prison or my body in my cell, and remember nothing else until I woke up terrified, drenched in a cold sweat and burdened with a case of the "flu" that lasted a month.

After that venture I gave up travelling in the present. My hobby of the past several years has been to imagine myself alive in different moments of the past. I read three books on a particular event to get a fix on its position. I then lay still and set the scene with layer after layer of people and trappings and backdrops until it takes on a life of its own.

I often go for high moments when daily life is sloughed off. The storming of the Bastille and Bobby Thompson's home run that gave the Giants the 1951 pennant are two favorites. More subtle pleasures in quieter places have come with Lewis and Clark along the Columbia River, and with the Doges of Venice as they met to manage the Mediterranean. And, when I've been surfeited with names and numbers, I've dropped straight back four centuries here in California to a time when the event of the season is a gathering under oak trees to trade obsidian blades, women, and dried fish; I've hunkered down in a dark sweat lodge and chanted while the heat purged me, and looked over this huge valley in May when the solid blinding gold of its massed poppies blew me right back to my cell.

Here and Now in Lagrimas state prison has little to recommend it. But, the thought persists in me, What if circumstances were ever such that some day in the future, a time traveller were drawn to come back and visit here? As I write here late at night to the music of intermittent moans, I feel around for another, someone much like myself, someone who has been to moments I'll never be able to reach.

2

He was known in Lagrimas as either z-1454 or the Fly; his mother's efforts at naming him had been overridden along with all her other good intentions. The series of numbers marked his place in the long line of apprehended California felons, while the insect tag arose, he hoped, from his activities as a writer of writs, complaints, and other briefs on behalf of his imprisoned brothers. It was said that he "stayed in their face," and was "always in their ear" or "buzzing around the bear's ass, looking for a bite."

He had been chagrined when the name threatened to stick. It lacked the resonance of Blackstone, for example, or the strength of Freight Train, or the dignity of Professor.

However, the passage of years made him aware of its accuracy as a metaphor for his legal efforts, and ever more mindful of the uses of insignificance. Were he called Clarence Darrow, those for whom he worked would blame him instead of the judges when their claims were rejected.

The series of events that blew the Fly out of his niche in Lagrimas began one hot August afternoon in 1974. He sat in his prison cell in boxer shorts, dripping sweat on legal documents while contemplating Richard Nixon's resignation.

Would new president Gerald Ford fulfill his part of the bargain and pardon Nixon for any and all crimes committed while acting as president?

Of course. Ford got the job because he was a team player. Nixon would press him to do it quickly, before either of them had a heart attack. The Fly had just decided that he would bet Walter Porter two cartons of cigarettes that Nixon would be pardoned within six months when Sgt. Arnold Huff waddled up bearing mail. Huff's fat, pale blotchy body was incongruously clad in the uniform of a gung-ho marine sergeant, three stripes to the sleeve.

"Swear to God Fly, they got to chop down a tree every day to keep you in paper."

The Fly walked past his cardboard filing cabinets and bunk to the cell door. The middle section of its metal bars was rubbed to a smooth glow by innumerable hands. "You got one from that Union of the Civil Dead that says Legal Mail on it." Huff tore open the envelope while ostentatiously turning his head so as not to sully the Fly's confidential relationship with the correspondent. He also tore the letter.

"God I'm sorry, Fly, *you* know that was an accident." Huff bent over to pick up the severed piece with a great flurry of groans and wheezes, and returned triumphantly with the missing portion. "You know, a lot of people got letters like that today."

Huff paused, and added, "I hope they're not trying to *start* something." The Fly turned and walked back to his bunk. "You ought to be a little more careful who you write to."

"I write to anyone who might write me back, Huff. I can't just walk down the street and talk to anyone I please like you can." The guard humphed a moment, apparently savoring his great social mobility, and lumbered on down the tier.

The Lagrimas staff always moved slowly. Fly thought their snail's pace was a function of great bulk and nothing to do other than drink coffee, smoke cigarettes, and wait twenty years for retirement, holding their breath lest they jar loose a riot. Huff could run, though, when the heat was on and the adrenalin drove him. The Fly remembered hearing gunshots fired shortly after he came to Lagrimas. Huff broke into a full-bore trot, presumably to take his post. Big men wearing military uniforms and leather shoes spit-shined by prisoners appeared from everywhere running toward the building's few doorways like overstuffed rats moving toward the only way off a sinking ship. In no time flat they were covered with sweat and puffing like steam engines; there was a terrific spill as two of them careened into each other near the door. The

Fly had laughed till he could not breathe, and laughed as hard each time the seasonal spectacle recurred.

The letter from the Union of the Civil Dead was signed by an attorney named Teresa Suchil, and aimed at "members or subscribers." He taped it together and read it:

> The Union of the Civil Dead is now attempting to gain for its members the right to hold regular meetings and function as a union inside Lagrimas State Prison. We intend to represent our members to the maximum extent legally allowed. The Union believes that current administrative practice does not extend to prisoners all rights to which they are constitutionally entitled, and will attempt to vindicate these rights before the prison administration, the legislature, the courts, and public opinion. I will visit any Union member who wishes to be a part of this effort. . . .

The Fly read the Union's paper whenever it made it through the hoops of prison censorship, and enjoyed its erratic stew of legal updates, doggerel pooping on officialdom, letters somehow smuggled out of prisons in rebellion, appeals for unity and organization, and odd features like a review of prime-time crime shows or a history of San Quentin in the 19th century when it was a jute mill owned by whoever happened to be warden. He kept his copy available in the law library for those who would read and return it. He promptly wrote a reply indicating a willingness to be visited, and sealed it just as Fred Johnson arrived at his cell, two minutes early.

Fred, an ideal client, was challenging his conviction for second degree murder more from a sense of thoroughness than from any expectation of results. He provided the Fly with all necessary papers and with answers to questions, and took care to comply with his part of their bargain: keeping his jailhouse lawyer from being disturbed.

After Fred finished a cursory review of his petition for a writ of Habeas Corpus and signed a declaration saying it was all true to the best of his knowledge and belief, he said, " 'scuse me, Fly, but do I spot a letter from the Union of the Civil Dead?"

"Yes you do."

"Are you gonna be seein' somebody from that organization?"

"Yes I am."

"I just mailed off my own letter askin' for their paper, an' joinin' up. If you of a mind to talk about your impressions after the visit, I be very interested in listenin'."

"Save me a pie this year—I'm not as fast as I used to be—and you can wring me dry on the subject."

"It's a done deal."

Other Black felons living in Lagrimas considered themselves Protestants, Catholics, businessmen, saxophone artists, scholars, sissies, revolutionaries, players, pimps, dreamers, or baad motherfuckers with the heart to kill and die. Many thought the Brotherhood—in which Fred Johnson was a high official—reactionary; more thought it silly. Still, no one, Black, White or Brown, laughed at it too loudly.

While working as the staff barber, Fred amiably sculpted the burr cuts favored by retired military men or the full look preferred by the younger set. Everyone the Fly knew believed that all Fred need do was open his mouth, and anyone within the far-flung Gulag of 13 prisons and dozens upon dozens of "camps" that made up the California Department of Corrections would be dead within twenty-four hours. His publicly displayed good will toward the Fly served as any good insurance policy should; it helped the Fly sleep at night.

The Fly had similar relationships among the other superpowers, and adhered to the sage advice of George Washington: no entangling alliances. In general, he found it useful to view the prison as a microcosm of the whole planet. Even though the stakes were forty cigarettes instead of the control of national monopolies, the same ruling passions of greed and fear were felt to the same degree. The differences were merely a matter of scale. Inside and out, dashes of altruistic behavior spiced life but did not sustain it. He had made himself a livable space. The advantages to "freedom" were so trivial in the Fly's mind that he saw no reason why he should bother to get out of prison.

Forty-eight hours of his week he spent in the law library. Created by court order five years earlier, it was a small room with books lining most of two walls. He sat behind a counter and doled out the material most vulnerable to having its juiciest morsels removed by avid researchers: certain legal how-to handbooks and reports of the most recent judicial opinions. He also gave advice to an endless stream of the legally confused.

The Fly found the law library miserably inadequate. A vocal minority of those who lived and worked in Lagrimas resented its very presence. When the prison was ordered to provide the books necessary to do legal research for those who could not afford a lawyer, the Warden bit into the space allotted to the regular library where the newspapers, magazines, Time-Life science books, and stories of scrappy little second basemen and hard-boiled private eyes were kept. After the legal victory (in which the Fly played no small part) there were fewer books to read, and queues of those too poor to afford a subscription to a daily paper became the rule rather than a rare exception.

The Fly's chief reason for responding to the Union's letter was diversion. He had so thoroughly polished his skills and buttressed his Lagrimas position that he was prey to the sieges of boredom that plague an overprepared life. Within a week he received a letter from Teresa Suchil telling him when she would appear.

Though the rules were always in flux for prison visitors, the ritual for those on the inside remained constant. The Fly walked from his wing down the central corridor and presented his ducat at the gate of the visiting wing. He was shown into an anteroom between staff offices where he took off all his clothing, had his few hairs parted, and bent over.

The anteroom was ferociously air-conditioned; he could not stop shivering. Lieutenant Sanchez, the man in charge of the visiting room, came out of an office to stare at him as he grabbed his ankles.

His asshole was scrutinized by Robinson, a man uniquely situated to do original work on rectal variations. Robinson had examined thousands during his tenure in the visiting anteroom closely enough to find several packets of drugs, a few razor blades, even a seven-inch knife, and been farted on more than once. Whether he had drawn any conclusions from this body of experience remained a mystery. He said nothing other than the affirmative grunt that allowed the Fly to pass through a second steel door. The Fly put on his denims and walked into the noisy tumult of the visiting room.

"Qué raro!" It was Sergio Magon and a woman who could only be his mother.

"Buenas tardes, Señora." The Fly bent at the waist and extended his hand.

"Buenas tardes, Señor. Mucho gusto. . . ."

"I've been telling her what a wicked old cheater you are for many years," murmured Sergio Magon. "What's happening, man? Who the hell would come see you?"

The Fly pointed to the row of small cubicles on the far wall next to the entrance gate. Teresa Suchil sat waiting, visible through the glass window that allowed staff to watch attorney-client meetings. He bowed again to Magon's mother and excused himself repeatedly, pulling slowly free from a tangle of politeness and courtesy. Teresa rose to greet him as he approached.

She was dressed in brown pants and a cream silk blouse. Blue-black tightly curled hair suggested India, but her skin was coppery rather than ashen, the same hue as the Aztec descendants with whom he lived, and it highlighted unexpectedly light green eyes flecked with gold around the pupils. She was taller than the Fly, and her body was far too fertile to suit him—large breasts, a waist that briefly narrowed before opening into firm, substantial hips. The Fly's ideal body type would bend in the slightest breeze; it was slender, willowy, male. The tiny room seemed horribly overcrowded as he sat across from her, their knees almost touching.

Teresa told him what the Union of the Civil Dead was trying to do: hold formal meetings in the prison to the same extent as did other groups, have elected prisoner representatives appear for prisoners at grievance hearings, meet and confer with departmental officials; to become a rather dilute union somewhat like those representing federal and state employees. She seemed tired, as if she had run her spiel once or twice too often. It was an effort to change the arbitrary nature of rewards and punishments in prison, she said. She was prepared to go to court.

Their cubicle soon became hot and stuffy. He kicked the door open and let in a wave of noise and cool smoke.

"How will all this come to pass?" he asked. The strategy Teresa described included much mailing of newspapers, news bulletins, and letters. He asked her leading questions about the current state of the law in regard to sending and receiving such materials to the press or elected officials, and whether one could send membership cards through the mail to prisoner members, and if ex-convicts were allowed to write to or visit current convicts. She was well acquainted with the latest developments in how the forms of expression were treated in a prison environment, and seemed happy to have questions to answer. Any rule that hindered the flow of information would be openly confronted and not circumvented, she said; means and ends are the same. She became more animated as they talked.

The Union was trying to cash in on the post-Watergate moment of open government by having a friend in Sacramento arrange a meeting with officials in the state capitol.

"Don't you think that will mess with your credibility?" asked the Fly.

"A little, but I think there's more to gain. They want to be seen as reasonable. Administrative meetings can accomplish in a few minutes what would take years to get a court to order. Any little change that comes from our meetings is a win for us, something to talk about. The more we meet the harder it will be for them to paint us as evil rabble-rousers when we go to court—and we will go to court once the meetings dry up and we've developed a bigger base of support in here. So long as we make real gains and aren't slowing down anywhere else, its worth the heat."

The Fly was intrigued, not because he thought any lawsuit could eliminate caprice from Lagrimas, but for essentially aesthetic reasons: in the circle of due process of law, it stretched the circumference of the Possible. A well-crafted, timely petition with a little bit of luck just might succeed.

His discomfort faded, and was replaced by suspicion. Precisely because she spoke intelligently about what she was actually thinking, he went on the attack.

"You sound good," said the Fly. "Let me tell you about the last time I listened to a silver-tongued lawyer."

The Fly sat with a genuine graduate of Yale Law School in the midst of Folsom's visiting room. The lawyer was eight inches taller than the Fly. His thick wavy brown hair and massive tanned body encased in a very expensive suit made him seem an overwhelming force. "That's it, then," concluded the lawyer. "An alliance between an association of jailhouse lawyers inside, and the Civil Rights Committee on the outside. You all are perfectly placed to gather the facts, declarations—we can mobilize support for you, make court appearances. We'll change the law, and you'll finally get the recognition for your work you deserve."

The Fly was ready to charge. Judges were expected, maybe even required, to follow the lead of guys like this, he thought. To hell with scraggly-bearded hippies, bull dykes, Venuses on the Half-shell in granny glasses searching for a doomed passion to lose sleep over—this guy looks like a real man! Appearances can be deceiving, he remembered, but that's the point—even if he is full of shit, any judge will take one look at him and start to bow and scrape. "Let's go for it," said the Fly.

The two of them fashioned a plan. The Fly agreed to set up a meeting of at least five jailhouse lawyers in the Folsom Law Library who would declare themselves a chapter of the Civil Rights Committee—the first chapter inside prison walls.

They would conduct a meeting to discuss current legal problems for one hour, and do the same each weekend. If the guards broke up the meeting, there would be their test case.

The Fly's colleagues were uneasy, but the need for open meetings rather than hasty exchanges of names and ideas while waiting to buy cigarettes was real, and the temptation of glory was great. Their first meeting was a smashing success, and became the talk of the Folsom yard. The jailhouse lawyers looked forward to their next meeting, and showed up from two to five minutes early.

The Fly called the meeting to order. "Are there any questions?" he asked. One hand went up. As if on cue, guards poured into the library, two for each convict. They shackled the Fly in the hallway, and dragged him to the Hole. Within two hours, still shackled, hands growing numb, he was taken through an infinitude of doors and placed on a bus.

The bus drove northeast through the foothills, over Sierra passes, and down into the desert above Reno. He slept that night in Susanville, and spent all the next day riding south, bouncing on a flat board seat, turning until he lost any sense of direction. His hemorrhoids returned on the third day of bus riding, and by the fifth his hemorrhoids had their own hemorrhoids. Finally, when the bones in his ass were on the verge of breaking through his skin, he landed in K-Wing of the Deuell Vocational Institute in Tracy.

He arrived at K-Wing in early December, and felt the cold breath of Christmas drawing closer and closer. The Holiday season is the most miserable time of year in any institution; echoes of celebrations remind every prisoner of his or her distance from the myth of America filled with happy families gathered around heaps of presents under evergreen trees. As the old year staggered towards its end, people who had cried out occasionally in the night took to moaning constantly. Screams and yells never stopped. Snarls of "Shut the fuck up!" from the disturbed who clung precariously to a separate peace only made the screaming louder.

Crazy men tore all their possessions and banged their heads against the walls. Some were stripped of everything, and then flung their excrement and piss through the bars at guards and anyone else within reach. Guards, who were forced to move down the hall to bring food and mail to men not allowed out of their cells, began wearing yellow slickers, and pissed into certain coffee cups destined for the cells of their greatest tormentors. After days of fitful sleep, his vision blurred and ears rubbed raw, in the very moment the Fly decided he was locked in Hell's own torture chamber for miscreants who had fallen into Satan's bad graces, things took a turn for the worse. K-wing was flooded with tear gas.

His eyes began stinging as he backed water out of the toilet at the foot of his bunk in order to breathe. He spent two hours hanging on the commode, his face buried as close to fresh air as he could push it, lips brushing cold white ceramic, listening to choked cries of rage and pleas for mercy and scuffling sounds of struggle as guards with gas masks entered the Wing. I shouldn't jump to conclusions, he thought; the bottom is always deeper than I can imagine.

"We were gassed twice more before the New Year. I spent the next two years working my way out of the Hole and up to the exalted position of law librarian." The Fly shivered as he remembered, and was pleased to see Teresa's face cloud over and her brows furrow deeper and deeper. He drove his point home. "And you know what? I never received one goddamned letter or visit from that pissant lawyer whose idea our meeting was, nor from anybody else in that committee. My question to you is, What the hell will you do when they throw me in the Hole because I get out front for this 'Union'?"

Teresa flinched, but she didn't buckle. "I can't promise that the same thing won't happen to you again, or that we could get you out if it did. I can and do promise that I'll do everything in my power to get you out. I'll file lawsuits, go to the state capitol, or stand out by the gate in the rain with a sign if nothing else works. I have no other work than what I'm doing right now, and nothing is more important for furthering this work than protecting the people inside who stand up for us." She looked him square in the eye, and he knew she meant it. "Well," he said irritably, sensing he had hooked himself, "I'll see."

He wanted to do better. "Actually, I'm interested." Her eyes sparkled as she smiled. "You know, you all are pretty lucky if I start moving in here—I know a lot of people." Her smile widened. "You lifted up the right rock this time," he said.

3

THE FLY THOUGHT HE WAS IMMUNE TO THE VIRUS OF ENTHUSIASM. Nevertheless, he tossed and turned the night away after Teresa's visit, busy with trial runs, imaginary conversations, probes for the soft spot. He saw in his mind's eye circumstances in Lagrimas so arranged that a handful of gestures could trigger wide and deep reverberations.

Lagrimas was built just after World War II, along with many other prisons, hospitals, universities, and schools that were the concrete embodiment of California's flush confidence. Its proper name was the Lagrimas Vocational and Correctional Institute, and for all I know, thought the Fly, its creators really believed they knew what would change criminals into reliable cogs in the machine. Without at least a pinch of sincerity they could not have persuaded anyone to give them so much money. Lagrimas was their centerpiece, designed to rehabilitate 2800 lost souls. Over twice that many were now jammed inside. The rehabilitative dream that inspired the prison had taken a terrible beating from 30 years of experience, as had its outward form. By 1974, its mint green Neo-Penal stucco exterior was crumbling.

Somewhere in his soul the Fly believed in the parity of all beings. He saw it every day in Lagrimas, where all the prisoners were males in identical blue denims. He also knew that there were differences between people so striking that it required faith and a good memory to place them as members of the same species. Most prisoners were inert mass. A few were levers.

A feeble breeze finally broke through the bars on his window, and blunted the heat. Faces paraded past by his mind's eye. He froze a few to look at closely. Fred Johnson would be invaluable, was already planning something. David Carruthers was effective, the only politically sophisticated radical convict the Fly had known wise enough to learn the ways of moving amongst prisoners.

He had met Carruthers in the library two years earlier. David was then a lanky and personable tow-headed southern boy who had been a skilled bomber on the outside. His trial had hit the popular and the legal press. He quickly conceded that the charred rafters of various army recruitment offices and banks up and down the West Coast were his handiwork, and went on to challenge the presence of any criminal intent by showing the reasonableness of his belief that the war was destroying the United States and Vietnam, and every means of stopping it short of violence had been exhausted.

A host of witnesses came to his defense: chaplains, war veterans burning with horror stories, legislators who described their struggles to regain their Constitution-given right to declare war. David testified on his own behalf. The jury found him guilty of the lightest charge possible—possession of explosives, six months to fifteen years.

Two days after his arrival Carruthers began pumping iron in the weight yard. In six months he swelled up from his lean student's frame to become a beefy mass of muscle. The Fly acknowledged the value in prison of strength and size, but privately considered the change as unfortunate. Carruthers made the Education Committee his base of operations. Lagrimas offered college classes and an "Associate of Arts" degree from nearby Grapevine Junior College. The program was a great favorite among veterans of the Vietnam war, who received the same recompense for going to school as their academically inclined brothers on the outside—$300 per month, a staggering amount of money in prison. The Groves of Academe were very crowded.

Shortly after Carruthers landed a full-time job as Education Committee clerk, the committee embarked on projects for the blind and illiterate with which no right-minded person could quarrel. Earlier in the summer, under the rubric of Adult Literacy, Carruthers introduced a disciple of Paolo Friere who had assisted in designing Cuba's literacy program. The lecturer argued passionately that reading was best taught when the text dealt with matters of real concern to the student. The Fly thought that the politics of most prisoners mirrored the politics of the outside world, with an anarchistic or reactionary gloss. At the same time, all prisoners loved to see somebody pull a fast one. Word got around that Carruthers was smuggling sneaky ideas into the pen, and the lecture series became a very hot ticket.

"Prisoners don't have any political consciousness," Carruthers once told him, "but they have a strong class consciousness. They know that if they steal on a big enough scale, they get a medal rather than a prison term." Carruthers talked to everybody. On his way to the library one day, the Fly stopped by a group of prisoners listening to an earnest conversation between Carruthers and a White Boy who weighed more than 300 pounds (naturally known as Tiny) about whether one would be required to wear motorcycle helmets under Communism. "Hell no." Carruthers was emphatic. "The State guarantees what you need so your desires can be freely lived out—it ain't supposed to be a baby-sitter." Carruthers' unique blend of libertarian communism sold rather well; but Carruthers could sell anything. He was a must for the Union.

No less important than finding proselytizers was neutralizing potential enemies. For example, Jack Slayton. Jack was not a man likely to become involved with something as disgustingly collective as a union—his image of unions was of pullulating termites devouring the foundation of a strong individual. He fancied himself to be Superman in blue, the Blonde Beast philosopher. Jack and the Fly had passed many hours playing chess and discussing the nature of existence. Neitzche was Slayton's philosopher, "the only man brave enough to look directly at the truth and write it down, even though it destroyed him." Thus Spake Jack.

Slayton was prone to stare into space for hours at a time, and was too moody and erratic to be the formal leader of the White Boys, a "gang" that imported and distributed goods and services into the prison, and purported to protect its members. However, on the strength of his reputation as one who had "killed some nigs," and his known use of big words, he was the ego ideal, the heart and soul of the organization. If he said something like, "This Union bullshit's got to go," two hundred crazed bikers and pimply tattooed drips looking for recognition would begin hunting for ways to make the Union go. The Fly resolved to see him as soon as possible.

Other faces and voices took their turn and stayed longer than they were welcome. The night never really cooled off, and its heavy air hindered his sleep. Uneasy dreams of feverish scrambling outside his cell soon woke him. Since the night remained dark and still, he picked up the same thread, and by the time of the wake-up call and First Count, the Fly had figured out a place to stand.

Fred Johnson came to see him in the law library the next day.

"Well?"

"What do you want to know?"

"Up or down?"

"I think its on the level. I'm going to help out, give certain people copies of their paper, write letters here and there, talk it up."

Johnson broke into a wide grin. "Glad to hear it! Fly, that woman's appearance here is the go-ahead sign."

"What do you mean?"

"Keep your eyes and ears open. I be talkin' to you."

Carruthers and his committee met once a week in the conference room just behind the library. On the day following his first visit with Teresa, the Fly saw Carruthers and Sergio Magon by the library door. Magon leaned against the door jamb as he talked; his thick eyebrows fluttered like a hummingbird and arched to the ceiling as he talked, and his baggy pants waved gently in a non-existent breeze. Carruthers stood on the balls of his feet, eyes bulging from his thick glasses, muscles bulging from his skin-tight t-shirt, ideas and energy oozing from his pores. The Fly walked up to them and made a Union pitch.

Carruthers nodded and hummed steadily as the Fly spoke. "I think an industrial democracy model would serve everyone better than a military model," he said. "Their newspaper is good."

"I want to make a Union in here," said Magon flatly. The Fly waited for an ironic undercut, but none came. "Let's go!" cried the Fly.

"What do you know about their leadership?"

"Not much. I did time with their President, Art Simpson. He was a motormouth Texan, an old blowhard thief. I can't see him leading anybody to the Promised Land, but he won't lead you into a closet and try to make you think it's a palace, either. Art could hold his mud." The Fly related what gossip he could remember of the ex-convicts known to work with the Union of the Civil Dead. "Hey," he said, hitting Magon on the shoulder, "What's with you, talking up a Union?"

"I was converted on the toilet two days ago," Magon explained.

"Huh?"

"I sat on the pot reading their paper, a paper I never gave much of a fuck about, when Scarborough came walking up and stared at me. I thought the motherfucker was kinda rude, so I asked him what the hell was he looking at, did he want a sample or what. He said, You better watch out and not get too close to that Union, so I told him I was goin' to be a goddamn Union steward, that we were gonna organize the entire joint and our first grievance was gonna be *him*. Scarborough is my role model, man. I figure if he don't like it, it's got to be good."

The Fly returned to his cell, gleeful at the willingness of Carruthers and Magon to join the fray. Carruthers would reach the prison's public people, and Magon could carry the word into otherwise inaccessible corners.

After the evening meal and count, the Fly walked down the long central hall to Jack Slayton's wing.

"Hello Jack." Slayton's lids were heavy. The Fly was afraid for a moment that he had been propelled by one of the White Boys' products into a parallel universe.

"Well, look who buzzed in! What's up, Fly?"

"The Union of the Civil Dead. They want to organize this place. I met their lawyer yesterday."

"So I hear."

"She's all right. I'm satisfied that they got some resources and aim to use them down here. Your feelings about unions are no mystery to me, so I'm not asking you to help. I know you could stop it in its tracks if you want to, so I'm asking you to sit this one out." The Fly wasn't positive that Slayton was so omnipotent, but he had always found the power of flattery to be as potent and mysterious as electromagnetism, almost impossible to misuse.

"You're late. That ham Johnson already came to see me." The Fly groaned. "He said, 'I don't like you, and I know you don't like me.' I appreciated his truthful opening. And he tells me, 'I respect you, though, as a leader. The leaders have got to do something.' Then he ran down about twelve 'problem areas' I think was his term." Jack smiled a razor-thin smile. "He wanted more from me than you're asking for. He wanted me to join the union and put out the word to others. He said the union was not about redistribution of the wealth—those weren't his exact terms, but I got his drift—but was for the purpose of 'dealing with conditions that affect everbody dressed in blue.' Who am I to be a spoilsport?"

The Fly gaped in surprise. "The Brotherhood seems to be fired up enough to take care of the details," said Jack. "Wanna play some chess?"

On Labor Day a young member of the Brotherhood came by the Fly's cell after dinner carrying a newspaper and a long row of signatures, and tried to sign him up for the Union. He left when the Fly showed him a membership card.

An hour later, Fred Johnson sat on the stool across from the Fly's bunk and talked. "What made me conceive the idea was that I read the Union's newspaper and saw that what they are saying is what I believe and what I could back. So, I approached the Minister and said Hey, we're having a lot of problems and feeling different kinds of pressure, and I feel if we scratch the Union's back the Union will scratch our back, and the way to do that is to show them what we can do—sign up hundreds of convicts to get the paper and join the Union. I proposed that I write and join first, and tell them what we would do. I figured it would have to be way out of the ordinary to get their attention since they must get thousands and thousands of letters. Then, we would have some of the brothers join, and go throughout the pen organizin' the rest of the convicts."

"What does the Minister think?"

"He's for it all the way."

"And how about Headquarters? Are they for it? Don't they still think that White folks are devils?"

Johnson sighed. "What a lot of people fail to realize is that once we become knowledgeable enough in our religion and our beliefs we don't always have to contact Chicago. We're taught that if we have an individual with leadership abilities in a particular area, he should be followed." A cell door slammed hard in the distance. Fly felt the wing reverberate through his thin mattress.

"You know, we're basically for what's right, regardless of the color factor. The color thing was used primarily to unite us, to bring about cohesion among a lotta beat down individuals with bad experiences and ideas that wanted some kind of rhetoric to unite on. When it came to *business*, though, we've always done business with anybody and everybody.

"We've grown a lot in the last fifteen years, enough to get away from being an oasis religion. We been gettin' pressure from the staff here that used to club us to death whenever they saw four of us in one spot cause they knew niggers only got together to plot on a riot. Now, they *like* us to get together. They want us to stay in our place packed off into a corner. We got to reach out in order to survive."

"What makes you think the Brotherhood can organize on any large scale? I don't need to tell you that a lotta people think you all are crazy." The dim cell faded another notch, and the Fly turned on his lamp.

Fred smiled, and leaned back against the concrete wall. "That's right, but we *have* got credibility. We've always been in touch with the heads of the various entities within the pens and said that if you run into any problems with the brothers, bring it to us and we'll take care of it. And we have. Gradually, by doin' what we said we would do, and not doin' what we said we wouldn't do, people have come to believe us even if they don't like us, and I mean the most hard-core peckerwoods. Even in times of great chaos, people gettin' stabbed and murdered all around, the Brotherhood ain't been touched in many many years."

The Fly leaned back, too; Fred Johnson was in an expansive mood. "I and others have explained to key people what we are up to, and everyone's response has been positive. All can see the need for something to deal with the hardships we all suffer. We ain't asked anybody to get out front on it yet. That comes later after they seen what we've done. I arranged to ditto off one thousand authorization slips copied out of the Union paper, got together with ten or twelve of the brothers, gave 'em the rap and spread them around the pen to go from cell to cell, job to job, clique to clique, tryin' to get people to join the Union. When I get a hefty number, I'll mail 'em in. The Union will see that we can take care of business, and if the staff sees us hooked up with the Union, even if its only an exchange of letters and visits, they'll think twice, three times, four times before comin' at us."

Johnson looked at the Fly for a moment with an appraising glint in his eye. "Early next year we're havin' our eighth anniversary service. We're going to open it up to people in the outside community, the top-level prison staff, and a few other convicts from the different nationalities. I hope you'll come."

The Fly was flabbergasted. The Brotherhood had made the word Separatist come to life inside California's prisons. No White or Brown person ever attended their religious services. Johnson filled the silence.

"You know how convicts are always noticin' each other, seein how people act under pressure, how they act in times of relaxation. A few men are the same through all situations. They're moved by themselves and by the things they believe in. A lot more people will look around and adapt themselves. They'll be a staunch soldier here, and off with the bunnies and the homosexuals over there. You know they just doin' whatever the environment calls for them to do to survive."

Two chattering prisoners walked by the cell. Fred glowered. "Then there are some individuals so concerned with goin' home that they would become rats and snitches to go home. They would eat the warden's shit with a tablespoon to go home. They would kill their own mothers to go home." A door slammed as he spoke. Screeches of laughter and an "Oh yeah!" echoed Johnson's words.

"We ain't all made to tolerate the same amount of pressure or go the same distance, but we can all use what we got wherever we are. Everybody knows its dirty and dangerous in prison, but precious few take the opportunity to become *steeled* that the penitentiary provides. Even within the Brotherhood, some of the brothers just move by like animals—ring the dinner bell and they drop the math book and the English book and the Bible and run to eat, goin' so fast they don't see what's to the right or the left or what they left behind."

Fred shook his head, stood up and stretched. "Well, I'm gonna let your ear cool off and go on back to my house."

"See you later," said the Fly. "You know I'm a pagan, but I wouldn't miss your service for the world if I get invited."

4

SERGIO MAGON HAD BEEN A CAUTIOUS CHILD. HE RARELY DID WHAT his friends dared him to do, preferring safety to a dubious honor. The important decisions in his life as a young man—to go to college in the San Joaquin Valley near his family, to marry Maria Fuentes, to work on the staff of federal anti-poverty programs in the late '60's, to use heroin when the programs closed—were not made because of their attraction, but because of the fearsome consequences of doing otherwise. He went to state prison in 1973 on various bad check and heroin possession charges. There, in 1974, the rewards of living dangerously came to him like a benediction, and he never looked back.

Early that summer he escorted a thin, mediumcomplexioned Black lover named "Sheba" to Saturday night movies one evening, to the general amazement and envy of the assembled. Interracial pairs were not unheard of in Lagrimas, but they were risky. Commingling of Blacks, Browns, or Whites offended plenty of people. The most recent victim of violence in Lagrimas had been Danny Liverette, a white man who was the "wife" of a Black man. Eddie Passoli had invited him to check out some new silk underthings; someone had stabbed Danny in the shoulder while he waited outside Passoli's empty cell.

Magon had never inspired fear. He was not thought of as one of the silent, deadly Chicano "homeboys" who never dreamed of dying in any way other than by a knife or gun. Nevertheless, he sat solidly on his folding chair in the first row, meeting the eyes of anyone who looked directly at them and occasionally touching or whispering to Sheba, who was "on"—a flurry of laughter, blushes, waves, and other flamboyances. The two paraded about thereafter without a whisper of problems.

It was Sheba who moved the Union to its first tangible victory. She (her pronoun of preference) worked as a nurse in the prison hospital. She was highly thought of by the patients, loved by the miserably ill as a Florence Nightingale who took her job far more seriously than any of the doctors. Chief M.D. Richards, a veteran of 25 years' state service, was an alcoholic. He favored bizarre theories of disease and health that centered, as did so many other aspects of Lagrimas life, in the asshole. His favorite operation was the hemmorhoidectomy. He performed them at the drop of a symptom, and in one infamous case, got his wires crossed and performed the operation on a prisoner scheduled to have his appendix removed. Richards struck more terror into the hearts of men in prison than any crazed convict or sadistic guard was ever able to muster.

A basic tenet Doctor Richards held was that anaesthesia somehow hindered the "natural process of recovery" from an operation. Loud lamentations of people he had opened with knives and left to their own devices filled the hospital wing. The role of pain-killers in his mind was to blunt resistance to an operation and to keep the victims quiet while it took place. The only respite from the good doctor was provided by his drinking, which led to an ever-increasing number of "sick days".

On the day before Halloween Sheba came sobbing over to Sergio's cell. "What's the matter, baby?" cooed Magon.

"Dr. Richards. He was *dead* drunk on his office floor at 11:30 today, and the only doctor on duty. David Umhofer's fever was *roaring* out of control and that young child Renfrew was *dying* of pain, and we could do nothing about it legally without his authorization. The door was locked. I had no idea what to do. If I fetch drugs from the cabinet I've committed a *capital crime*. We banged on the door and banged on the window right above him. He was laid out clear as a bell between his waste basket and desk. Finally, Savoy had the bright idea of calling Doctor Young, but no one was home. Doctor Richards was *all there was*."

"What did you do?"

Sheba smiled a wicked smile. "I broke the window. Let them *hang* me, I don't care. The old fool staggered up and we had some antibiotics and Demerol where they needed to be in no time flat."

Magon chewed a figurative weed for a moment, as he was prone to do, and said, "Sweetie, we must get rid of the doctor or something will happen to you."

"It's *way* past time."

"You will have to play a key role in this project if we want to succeed. I suppose, though, that you are too frail for the job."

"Listen, buster, I've got more *balls* than any ten of the strutting balloons parading around this pen who would pop at the sight of a prick. What must I do?"

Two weeks later Magon came to the law library with a thick package containing a list of gross violations of standard medical practice detailed and signed by seventeen of the nineteen MTA's, the prisoners who effectively ran the hospital; affidavits signed by Richard's patients attesting under penalty of perjury to the truth of the charges; xeroxed copies of medical records that supported the claims made, either directly or by eloquent omission; and five sets of legal papers, civil rights lawsuits filed in federal court naming Richards as the defendant. Two of the lawsuits had apparently settled, with money awards to the prisoner plaintiffs. The Fly was mightily impressed.

When Teresa reviewed the package with the Fly on Wednesday before Thanksgiving, she whistled. After their visit, the Fly told everyone he knew that the Union was going to dump Richards. Four weeks later, on the eve of Christmas, Richards tendered his resignation.

Teresa later told Magon the Union had presented correctional officials in Sacramento with an alternative—either get rid of Richards, or the Union would file a series of lawsuits day by day against him, each accompanied by press releases describing Richard's reign of crackpot drunken butchery. "They claimed to be grateful for our restraint, and said they had already decided to bounce him—having to settle out of court twice triggered their employee warning alarm."

"Do you believe them?"

Teresa shrugged. "Who cares?"

Interest in the Union multiplied in the wake of Richards' overthrow, and another recruiting drive netted several hundred signatures. Union organizers travelled over Lagrimas like circuit riders that winter. Magon talked to Chicanos from Los Angeles and San Jose and the Central Valley, and staked out a position for the Union separate from neighborhood watch and business pursuits. Carruthers worked among "honor" prisoners, and the Fly distributed papers and information from the law library.

Prison guards were struggling for recognition as a public employees' union at the same time, and Magon developed a taste for talking to them. "I think a union for prisoners would bring more safety to the pen," he would say, "and I know it would help you guys organize. I mean, nobody is going to let a bunch of convicts have a better organization than their keepers. The more formal recognition we have, the bigger base you guys have to get what you want. Think about it." He left them scratching their crewcuts. Carruthers ingratiated himself with two of the institution's senior administrators, and made an enthusiastic recruit of the prison's high school English teacher.

The lifeline throughout for the Union organizers was Teresa Suchil. She came once a month and visited six people one day and six the next, always blending new people and the four regulars: Fred Johnson, David Carruthers, Sergio Magon, and the Fly. They each saw her every other month. Work taken on during these visits structured their time in between. Six months after her first visit, the Union was far from official, but it had become a fact of Lagrimas life.

In late November, the Brotherhood sent invitations in every direction to the "First Memorial Open House Service," to be held on Saturday, February 1, 1975. "Man, they invited every jazz musician, relief pitcher, nose guard, power forward, blues player and funk singer within 200 miles, all the Brotherhood ministers and Black politicians for miles around, all the big brass in this pen, everybody in the Union of the Civil Dead, and six convicts!"

Speaking was the Fly's colleague and chief rival for legal business, a salt-and-pepper, kinky-haired old codger named Walter Porter. Walter and the Fly had exchanged a few barbed words over the years, but time and steady work habits bumped them each up to the top of the jailhouse lawyer heap. They had even taken to referring clients back and forth who had problems that the other knew best. Upon receiving his invitation in the mail, Walter promptly went to the law library to talk about it with the Fly.

"I'm damned if I'm going to their little pageant," Walter said, swelling with indignation. "I've always regarded that bunch as a pack of superstitious loonies, and they know it. True, they don't spend all their time gettin' stoned and layin' up in their bunks dreamin' about all the pussy they're gonna get on the streets, but have you checked out that crazy shit they believe in? Ooga booga! You know what I think, now that the Founding Crackpot (he rolled his eyes heavenward) is dead."

"He's dead?"

"Passed on to become a voluptuary in the sky. Its a brand new day Halleluyah! His son is the new supreme Honcho—evidently he inherited the job along with the living room chairs—and he wants to open things up. This shindig is a move in that direction."

"Why don't you want to support it? They've been the motor behind the Union. Looks like a good change to me."

"Because I don't have a religious bone in my body. The Warden's gonna pull the chain on 'em anyway, no doubt about it."

"Oh, come on. Treat it like an alternative to the Saturday night movie. Dave Carruthers is coming, and he's a stone Communist."

"Another religious nut!"

"Hunk Dayton's coming, and he's a football player."

"Still another religion! I can see it all now, all the cranks for miles around comin' to celebrate the fact that one of their own who has been off in a corner invites all the *other* cranks to come and see their precious private parts!" Walter thundered on for another minute, and fell into a smirk. The Fly made another cast.

"Tyrone Edwards is coming and Art Simpson, and Teresa Suchil. The *warden* is coming, you sorry old motherfucker. If you've got a hair on your ass, you'll come, too."

"Not a chance!" he roared.

"You know who's going to preach?"

"Harlan Johnson. Skinny little nigger from Oakland, got a real big voice."

Walter sat still. The Fly paused, and asked, "Think he'll put it to the Warden?"

"Hmmmm. Probably he'll suck up and slaver all over the guests and the Warden, and tell them all what heroes they are for turning out. He might not, though. The boy does have some grit in him."

"Fred Johnson invited me, and he's got more grit than Muscle Beach. It sounds like the event of the season in here. It's not like we could pass it up in favor of the opera, you know. They *invited* you, you old blockhead. I've never known you to be rude and stupid at the same time. Besides, how are you going to be able to trash it if you weren't even there?"

Walter almost bit. "Good point, Fly," he said after a moment's silence. "It'll hurt me to have all those potential customers hanging around your cell to get what they think is the real story. But no go."

At the year's end the Warden circulated a new "open door" policy in the course of setting out the conditions of the Brotherhood's Memorial Service. He stunned the White Boys who were grumbling about the privileges extended to the Brotherhood by announcing that their long-time dream, a Motorcycle Show, would take place inside the prison in the spring.

Reaction to these moves was divided between those who thought the Warden was acting to preempt the growing power of the Union and those who thought that it was all a cock-tease, that outsiders, particularly ex-convicts, would never be allowed on the prison grounds. The latter group gained adherents when, two days before its scheduled date, the Warden abruptly cancelled a Christmas music show that had been months in the planning.

The Brotherhood wasn't talking much during the week before the service, but everyone else was. Rumors flew that a strong minority (or even a majority) of Brotherhood members were uneasy with the Union connection, and unhappy over the prospect of a religious service attended by Whites, Browns, and heathens. Carruthers and the Fly were the only White convicts invited, and Magon the only Brown; all were avidly sought after. The law library filled with browsers squeezing the Fly for news. Late in the week a kidnap plot aimed at the Warden floated through the prison. No one professed to believe it but everyone repeated it. Friday's favorite rumors centered on a coup within the Brotherhood and an imminent cancellation of the service. There was also much discussion of Union founders Art Simpson and Tyrone Edwards, who had been in prison within living memory of several convicts, and Raphael

Matus, a legend as the only known ex-felon college professor. They were said to be either rolling in barrels of free foundation money, good drugs, and gorgeous co-ed volunteers who wanted nothing more than to type all day, cook and wash dishes all evening and make love all night; or slaving away ruining their eyes and backs over broken mimeograph machines in a cold and leaky San Francisco garret, courting pneumonia on behalf of the ungrateful unworthy.

A thick Tule fog came ten days before the service, and penetrated the Fly's thin skin to his bones. He hated Tule fogs. They were nothing like the beautiful billowy coastal fogs. Tule fogs materialized out of the air and hung motionless, a pervasive curtain of numbing cold that trapped fumes and grime and blocked all visibility. Travelers along valley roads either crept slowly in the wake of highway patrol cars or piled up in crashes involving dozens of vehicles. The Tules meant limited movement and tense times in Lagrimas. Gun tower guards could not see the ends of their rifles, let alone any escaping convicts.

The rains returned the night before the big day, and washed the air clean of fog and suspended waste. The Fly walked a half mile down the long hall from his wing to the auditorium, and showed his ducat to the guard at the door. He swiftly scanned the auditorium as he entered. Turnout was fair. The Union appeared in force. The Brotherhood's outside community ministers, starched and dressed in gray three-piece suits, sat in a clump close to the warden, who brought an entourage, but few of the invited stars came out.

Exactly one hour had been allotted for the Brotherhood's event. The first ten minutes passed in a silence broken only by echoing coughs, while two hundred or so people sat shuffling on folding chairs, waiting in front of an empty stage.

A slightly built blue-black man emerged from the stage's left side. He walked back and forth several times before he spoke, staring at the floor with his hands behind his back. Suddenly he broke his reverie and approached the microphone. "Brothers and sisters, welcome!" His voice boomed among the exposed rafters, and seemed to come from everywhere at once. "We are deeply grateful to our guests for making possible this breakthrough day.

"Today, the Brotherhood celebrates its strength by making a part of our religious service our indissoluble connection with the world. Well behind us lies the bad times, when we were mocked, scorned, despised, yes, even *beaten* because of our essence. Our very essence, our intrinsic nature, was a hardship, a lead weight, a chain holding us down!

"When we began to gather together our separate, isolate drops of battered Black individuality and coalesced into a great dark cloud of anger and power, laws, rules, regulations were thrown together and aimed straight at us, brothers and sisters, straight at our hearts.

"We overcame those obstacles, we blew them away like straws in the wind, and how did we do it? Not by hope. Not by *wishin'*, but with the solid rock of faith.

"We believed in ourselves, in each other. We believed in God and knew that the Almighty was with us. *Nothin'*, not even life itself, was worth turning on our own selves, abandoning our brothers, putting God aside—especially not a little bit of discomfort for some White folks made uneasy by Black people looking at each other for a change rather than studyin' the White man.

"By our faith and the perseverance it made possible, we earned the right to be here today, with one another in God's presence. Our faith has moved mountains, brothers and sisters, and now, its callin' on us again. The time has come to change the river's course. It will take all your strength and mind and heart, but God is with us.

"The time has come to fall back down to the earth and intermingle with *all* the currents of humanity. There is no way we can achieve alone a world in which the majesty of the law guarantees a careful consideration of each one of us when we have a grievance, or when the community believes we have aggrieved it. There is no other way to a world where abundance can be created and enjoyed without guilt or envy. The time has come to expand our identities, to live in a world of multiple realities. The time has come!

"Now, God wants all you got, but rest assured the Almighty doesn't want the impossible. You already know how to do it, you've already always done it.

"You've lived as a man, as a Black person, as a prisoner. You've acted like a hardass tush-hog *convict* in Folsom prison, and like an easy-goin' *inmate*, fantasizin' about the future instead of lookin' behind your back, when they moved you to Chino or Camp Redwood. Everything in its season, brothers and sisters."

The Minister dropped his voice an octave and leaned into his audience. "By turning inward we have gained respect. We've earned that little bit of fear that is every man's birthright. All members of the Brotherhood on the outside are now reaching out and workin' with the people around them. Our task here, in prison, is to take our fate with both hands, use our time to master the skills we will need to survive, to flourish, and work together with every man locked up in here behind these walls to build a house of justice for *all*."

The Minister searched the faces of the crowd as his voice reverberated through the hall; when silence replaced its echoes, he said softly, "God bless you," and left the stage.

The Fly walked past four Black men dressed in starched and pressed blues standing behind tables covered with white tablecloths, cake and pink punch, eager to serve. Just behind him swept the warden, closely followed by his followers; a curt nod to the servers repeated five times, and the prison administration was gone. The rest of the crowd, accompanied by several guards, stayed to eat, drink, and talk for the remainder of the allotted hour. The Brotherhood prisoners were filled with enthusiasm and the uniqueness of the moment, while their outside ministers stood stiffly in three-piece suits, tangled by mixed feelings, saying little beyond minimal pleasantries.

Teresa introduced the outside Union members to inside Union members. The Fly noticed that Art Simpson was considerably thicker than when the Fly had last seen him in Folsom. Art still had the same steady flow of words and the same bray of a laugh. His lumpy red face was saved from dullness by quick light blue eyes. Raphael Matus came in a long cashmere coat. The only ex-convict known to the Fly who had gone on past prison to Academia and the publication of several books, Raphael was acting like he had somehow landed in Lagrimas by accident. Tyrone Johnson, a big beachball of a Black man, floated easily through the crowd, and there were a couple of women he had never seen . . . the Fly pulled back toward a wall, and heard the voices and laughter blend into a dull roar that drowned out separate parts, leaving the anteroom full of loud noise and mouths moving apparently without effect.

Fred Johnson, his face beaming, was the only other person not standing in a knot of people. The Fly made a thumbs-up sign, and saw a thin, pale, absolutely beautiful boy with long black hair standing in a group with Art and Carruthers. The young man listened attentively, dark

eyes moving back and forth to the speaker, occasionally darting over to
a listener to gauge the speaker's impact. He was surely a Good Boy, very
different than the Bad Boys the Fly knew so well. Bad Boys, God bless
them, had no way to lunge from one moment to the next other than sheer
desperate improvisation, while Good Boys waited politely in the back-
ground until the day when they drew near and told you they now had
title to the house you lived in and owned the clothes on your back. . . .
The young man was magnetic; the Fly felt himself being drawn over.

"Hey, Legal Eagle, you're lookin' good!"

"So are you, Art."

"Meet Robert Chime, Chief Assistant and main letter-writer.
Couldn't live without him." The young man blushed as Art clapped him
on the back, and the Fly shook his hand. Teresa walked over, and they
spent the remaining twelve minutes of the gathering talking in fragments,
basking in the day's events.

5

THE COUP THAT MADE THE UNION OF THE CIVIL DEAD KNOWN TO most of California was struck by an unlikely by-product of the Lagrimas furniture factory: Theodore "Chilly" Morris's left ring finger.

The factory occupied most of a long, tall shed outside the main prison building. Nothing like a safety inspection ever occurred there except in a small room by the entrance created especially for that purpose. In the main shop, noise roared unabated, sharp steel sawblades whirled unguarded. Electric cords, butt ends of wood pieces, sawdust, oil, and loose paper covered the floor. Fifty-five-gallon drums jerry-built on skate wheels ploughed through the debris carrying goods back and forth, or sat empty for days in the center of passageways.

Chilly Morris came to the Fly's cell in the summer of 1975 carrying a small white box, looking for legal miracles. The Fly and Sergio Magon were playing chess on the bunk. Morris sat on the stool cradling his package, and told his tale.

Morris had grumbled and groaned when he was assigned to the furniture factory the previous fall, but he complied. In 1969 he had refused, and did not see the parole board that year. "I worked on the ripsaw for a while, but didn't get along with this guy I was workin' with, so I asked Bill Doyle the supervisor to move me. He stuck me on the hand jointer, right there in the cuttin' and millin' part of the factory where I worked before. I got seat blanks from the rip saw next to me, boards about three feet long, four inches wide, inch and a half thick. I'd run 'em over a real high speed saw blade that didn't poke up more than a thirty-second of an inch out of a steel table, to make their surface smooth, even, and straight. Then I'd hand the board on over to the planer.

"The way it was done was to use a push stick to push to board with your right hand, but the only way to control the board was to put your left hand on it about three inches from the end of the board and hold it steady. Well, the boards was always buckin' on me because they would send me junk ends, ratty old wood that was warped, or too small, or had knots in it. Boards like that would kick back on you when they hit the blade. This spring I had a glove on my left hand to keep from gettin' splinters. A board kicked back on me and my glove got caught up in the blade—my fingertip got cut. They told me not to wear no more gloves."

"Who's They?"

Chilly snorted. "Bill Doyle the supervisor. After that, I started gradin' the wood that was comin to me, lookin' at the boards to see if they're OK, and gettin' rid of the junk ends. Doyle put the kibosh on that one day. He told me the people on the rip saw would grade the wood, and I was to just smooth it and send it. I sneaked looks at the boards anyway, but I came across one that had a hell of a knot in it that passed me by. It was the one that got my finger."

The Fly and Magon both turned to look at the little box Morris brought with him, the kind that people use to take potato salad home from the delicatessen.

"What happened?"

"I was pushin' the board through. The blade hit that knot and kicked the board back. My left hand was pushin' down to keep the board on track, and went on down into the hole in the table where the blade was. That blade just sailed through my ring finger like it wadn't even there. My hand jumped out of the hole with that one finger hangin' by a thread of skin. Got me right here at the first joint."

He held up his left hand; a swollen lump of dirty bandage sat where a finger had been. As Chilly pulled a cigarette from his shirt pocket with no apparent loss of dexterity, Magon moved quickly to offer him a light.

"They pulled off one of the men from the ripsaw and sent him with me over to the hospital."

"You walked?"

"That's right. We finally got there, and didn't find no doctor around nor even any lights that worked for 45 minutes. They had one who finally showed up and tried to save it, but it was no go. When they told me there wadn't nothin' they could do, I said, 'where's my finger?', and the doctor and the nurse snuck a quick look at each other. That's when I knew I wanted my finger back. They didn't want to let me have it, but I said, 'It's my damned finger, ain't it? I never gave it to you or anybody else, and I sure as hell never threw it away.' I told 'em the least they could do if they couldn't sew it on was to go find it and give it to me, and by God they did. Here it is."

He opened his box and pulled out a shriveled, bluish thing recognizable as a finger because of the nail, a rough-edged nail that still sheltered a line of dirt and sawdust along the cuticle.

Magon's eyes gleamed with a preternatural brightness. He swallowed hard, and said as off-handedly as he could, "Let me see that." Morris was forthcoming. Magon contemplated the finger for a moment, and said, "Hey, Chilly, you know what . . . we might be able to do something with this little pickle."

After Morris left, Magon followed. "I got to get this to Carruthers," he explained. The Fly opened his mouth to protest, but remembered that he was a knight and two pawns down. "Good luck," he yelled to the quick-moving Magon. The finger lay on ice in the mess hall until Carruthers could get it to the English teacher, who packed it out with test papers and iced it in his freezer where it marked time very slowly until Teresa stopped by to pick it up on the way back from her next trip to Lagrimas.

Aaron Brenner, the Union's man in Sacramento, had gone to the state capitol in 1969 after passing the California Bar Examination to lobby on behalf of farmworkers, and had never left. His most recent of several poor-paying jobs working for poor people was with the County Legal Aid Society. During the winter Aaron had drafted a bill for the Union of the Civil Dead abolishing California's Civil Death Statute, and found a senator to carry it. The bill sailed through the more conservative upper half of the legislature, but bogged down in the Assembly Committee to Protect the Public Safety, whose members were miffed that the bill, with which they ostensibly agreed, did not have their name on it.

"But if you guys start a bill like this," Aaron wailed over a bacon and tomato sandwich to the chief committee staff member, "the Senate would swat it like a fly as a piece of liberal criminal coddling!"

"The committee believes that this kind of legislation is what it knows best, and anything from the senate requires our very close scrutiny before we can send it to the floor. Its 3-2 against you right now. The members want to hold it over a year. We're looking at big bills in juvenile justice and a mandatory prison law for burglars. Your effort is simply one of a hundred we don't have time for."

"A year is a very long time."

"Take it easy. They'll pass something out."

"Shit!" cried Aaron in exasperation.

"Look, I'm sorry, but that's how it is."

Aaron left the capitol cafeteria and walked rapidly back to his office three blocks away toward the wrong part of town, indifferent to the scorching heat. In his doorway, clinging to the shadows, sprawled the dishevelled body of a man whose face had been broiled to a scarlet crisp by the summer sun. With a practiced eye, Aaron noted the man's regular breathing. He slipped a card with the United Displaced Men's Association's address and phone number into the man's jacket pocket, and stepped over him and up the stairs. One of his many messages was from Teresa Suchil in San Francisco. He promptly called her, and learned of Chilly Morris' finger.

"Is there a Union meeting this Wednesday?"

"Yes."

"I'm coming down. Leave plenty of time on the agenda for that finger."

"Don't worry, it'll be on the table."

Meetings of the Union of the Civil Dead were held in Art and Myrna Simpson's dining room on the second floor of an old three-story San Francisco building that would be called "Victorian" in later years when Real Property replaced Utopia as the axis of the city's imagination.

One glimpse at the first floor office made clear why meetings took place upstairs. The chaotic, cavernous room, formerly a butcher shop, was filled with telephones, overflowing file cabinets, an old printing press, great piles of newspapers that varied in tone from newly minted white through dingy yellow to moldering gray, and cluttered desks on which wire baskets sat, smothered by requests, complaints, invitations, and demands congealed on reams of insistent paper.

In the dining room, bay windows opened to the east, revealing a sliver of the last ship yards on the San Francisco side of the bay and the blank wall of the store next door; south windows looked over the lower deck to a neighbor's weatherbeaten fence. The room was light, airy, and private. The room's centerpiece was the dining room table. The blonde table, made by Art shortly after his last release from prison, was a long heavy rectangle lightened by rounded corners and the radiance of its ash color.

Aaron clapped his hands. "How the hell did you get your hands on that thing? My God, it's disgusting."

Theodore Morris' finger was the table's centerpiece.

It rested on a blue platter surrounded by dry ice, pointing toward the ceiling. Fumes curled upward, as if they understood and were following directions.

"When is our bill up for a hearing?" asked Myrna.

"In exactly two weeks, on June 28. We're in trouble."

Aaron explained the dynamics that were pointing to a year's delay.

Raphael frowned. "One year from now won't help us."

The refrigerator in the kitchen groaned as it turned again to its work of cooling, and the chandelier overhead dimmed in sympathy. Art Simpson looked off into space, and saw a giant pincer movement of powerful forces converging. From the legislature came the repeal—under a Union banner—of the hated law that forbade convicts from suing, marrying, signing contracts, willing property, reading what they chose, all the basic prerogatives of adulthood; and from the lode of convict energy at Lagrimas flowed a lawsuit establishing the Union's presence inside. . . . Art's right leg was tapping rapidly, like a sprinter unable to stay in the starting blocks. "Let's get on every nag we got and ride as hard as we can. Any reason why not, Aaron?"

Aaron shook his head very deliberately. "Not that I can see."

Robert Chime could not sleep the night before the committee hearing. He sighed with relief when his alarm sounded, and rode his bus across town as the morning turned from black to gray. Raphael, Teresa, Art, and Myrna waited at the Union building, and they all drove up the river to Sacramento, shedding layers of clothing as they went.

Aaron met them at his office. He had scheduled a room in the state capitol for a press conference. After a review of what lay ahead, they walked to the capitol for lunch. Robert was growing nervous. "How many people will show up?" he asked.

"Who knows? Depends on what else is happening at the same time." Two reporters waved at Aaron and approached them in front of the Capitol elevator. Aaron spoke, and introduced them to the Union members. They all crowded into the elevator and rode to the top floor. As they left the elevator Aaron smiled. "It looks like we'll have a full house. I put out the word that one of Morris' extremities had been severed and would be on display, but neglected to specify which one."

Robert sat silently while those around him talked to visitors as they ate. Teresa's eyes were dancing, her laugh easy and escalating. She caught Robert staring at her, and squeezed his knee under the table. He flushed wildly, and lowered his eyes while sensing each separate tingle in his leg where she had touched him. Did she know that he thought about her for hours every day? She must; he was so damned transparent around these people, forever flushing and paling. Whatever had happened to the detached, masked person he had always been before, at home and on campus? Teresa's hair had lengthened until her curls swung like jungle vines in a tropical storm when she turned her head—he found himself staring at her face again, and abruptly bolted from the table.

Robert roamed the halls of the Capitol until he realized with a burst of panic that he had lost all sense of time. He ran to the hearing room and pushed his way past a dozen people to a seat down front. Then, as his breath returned, he looked around at the theatrical setting of hundreds of cushioned seats sweeping in rows down towards a brightly lit, elevated crescent table at which eight men sat. A plain table, bearing only a microphone and water pitcher, waited in a supplicant position below.

On the far left of the crescent was a dark, rigid man with a lined face who resembled a slab of wood more than a human being. In the center was a florid, round-faced fellow more porcine than Porky himself, and next to him was an inflated caricature of a man who surely would float away any second—Robert could not see any of the eight commitee members as real people. Blinking and squinting were no help. Then, he saw Art, Teresa and Raphael in a little corral to the left of the small table below. A Deputy Attorney General left the corral and went to the small table, where he urged the committee to delay acting on a change in standards relating to who was eligible for bail.

"Third item on the agenda is Senate Bill 109, a bill purporting to amend Penal Code section 2499 to abolish the so-called Civil Death Statute." He was not too late. "Will anyone wishing to testify for or against please come to the front. Bear in mind that the committee is familiar with the bill and has staff summaries at their fingertips. Brevity is an important part of effective testimony."

"The most important part," said the Balloon, who leaned forward and spoke so close to his microphone that the audience was jarred by an abrupt increase in volume. Robert felt chilled.

Raphael testified first. He began by saying he was an ex-convict, and then listed his publications, positions, and awards. In a building where all honor goes to the surface self and the good example officially reigns, the committee members ceased their chatter for a moment and made small noises of deference to the Rehabilitated Man. Raphael spoke of the history of Civil Death Laws since their first use by the Roman Empire, and presented evidence that their repeal by the majority of states had led to no discernible problems. His substantive testimony lasted not quite as long as his recitation of qualifications.

Teresa identified herself as the attorney for the Union, and detailed the legal implications of each subsection of the old law and the effect of the new law's passage. Art followed, welling with excitement, and took a white cardboard box with him to the microphone.

"Ladies and gentlemen. My name is Art Simpson. I'm an ex-convict and the president of the Union of the Civil Dead. I thank you for the chance to speak. I hope to make you aware, not of law history or legal terminology, but instead of what the law means, by showing you something that it produces with a terrible regularity."

"You have an exhibit for the committee, Mr. Simpson?" asked a member.

"Here it is."

A staff member walked down from the crescent desk and took the box from Art. He presented it to the member seated on the far right, who gave the box a perfunctory glance and passed it on. The roiling murmur of voices and movement, unbroken since the hearing began, grew louder.

The second member opened the box. His face screwed up in puzzlement, and he reached gingerly inside as Art began speaking. After a few seconds of intense scrutiny he dropped the box as if it were a hot coal and cried, "What the hell is it?" The box fell to the floor, and a small dark object spilled out and bounced down beneath the platform.

"The left ring finger of Theodore Morris, a prisoner and an employee in the Lagrimas State Prison." Art leaned into the microphone. "Mr. Morris lost his finger while working on unsafe, illegal equipment that has already cost two other men fingers in this calendar year, and has maimed a dozen other prisoners that we know of within the last four years."

The two staff members came down and around in front of Art to search for the dropped object. The Sergeant of Arms joined them when they dropped to their hands and knees and began looking beneath the crescent desk and the table at which Art sat. Half the committee stood and leaned as far forward as they could, while the other half remained studiously indifferent. The murmur grew to a buzz.

"Morris will never speak to me again if you all lose his finger." Pockets of laughter opened. The old Sergeant emerged from the pit in front of Art with the finger and its box, and calmly put the box back on the crescent desk. No one touched it.

"What can Mr. Morris do about the loss of this finger?" Art's voice rose. "He can't do a damned thing, if you'll excuse me, because he gets no workers' compensation and because he is civilly dead he can't go into court and sue. There ain't *nothin'* he can do, and if the foreman tells him that he's got to show up on the same job running the same saw the day after he gets out of the hospital, he's got to do it. If he doesn't do it, he doesn't get a parole date, and because Mr. Morris was convicted of burglary his indeterminate sentence runs from twenty months to life in prison, so if he doesn't get a parole date he'll rot in Lagrimas state prison. So, Mr. Morris is working right this minute on a saw that has no guards at all on it in spite of California's requirement that table saws have safety guards, and is putting what fingers and life he has left in jeopardy.

"Gentlemen, if you'll allow me to be blunt and to tell the truth straight out, you all are sitting right now in chairs made by slave labor that is working in conditions not fit for a dog. So long as fingers like the one before you are not worth a penny in the eyes of the law, that furniture factory—a multi-million dollar a year operation—will continue to eat human limbs and grind men into sawdust. Unless you have questions, I have nothing else to say."

6

Art had accomplished a feat rarely seen in legislative hearing rooms—he quieted the audience. The silence stretched for several seconds, and was finally broken by a swell of applause.

The Chairman banged his gavel and declared, "The committee will stand in recess." He promptly exited stage left midst agitated buzzing, followed by all his brethren. The buzz became a roar as all stood up and rushed toward the doors.

In the press room a knot of people surrounded Art, Raphael, and Teresa. Electronic media workers shoved microphones at them, asked them questions, and yelled commands to the bearers of lights behind. Newspaper reporters elbowed their way ahead of lobbyists for church groups and ex-convicts from the Sacramento area. Like logs burning on a cold mountain night, those who testified were of inestimable value for the moment; the morning after, they would be worth no more notice than smoldering ashes.

Aaron and his wife Marie cooked hamburgers for their guests on a crumbling brick fireplace at the end of their deep back yard in downtown Sacramento. They drank cold beer under the shade of a black walnut tree and marvelled at two apricot trees staggering under the weight of thousands of ripe, juicy fruits; "our little balls of bliss," said Aaron as he placed a crutch under a limb that could not sustain the weight of all its gold.

Robert stayed inside the dark, cool house playing with the television set, until he saw a young man's head say:

"Dramatic testimony before the Committee to Preserve the Public Safety today. We'll have that story and more when we return."

"It's on!" he yelled to the back yard, and everyone flocked into the living room.

"Today, in a dramatic moment before the Assembly Committee to Protect the Public Safety, a spokesman for a group calling itself the Union of the Civil Dead presented the committee members with a finger which he stated had been cut off as a result of illegal and unsafe equipment in the Lagrimas State Prison furniture factory.

"Union President Art Simpson claimed that the very chairs on which the committeemembers were sitting had been made in the prison under unsafe conditions. The Channel Two news team has learned that the chairs were indeed manufactured in Lagrimas, which sold 3.5 million dollars worth of furniture to the state of California last year. Kim Flint has the story."((CUT to Kim in front of the capitol))

"Bob, as far as we can determine, a minimum of five people within the past three years have lost fingers, or in one case, an entire hand, while working at either the metal or wood furniture factory at Lagrimas.

"A committee of private businessmen and labor leaders is charged with reporting annually to the legislature on prison industries. This committee has never been inside the furniture factory on any of its six visits to the prison. Seymour Gannett was named to the board by the governor in 1972, and has toured the facility twice. Mr. Gannett talked to us this afternoon."((CUT to Kim and Mr. Gannet, standing in front of the Prison Industry Office in downtown Sacramento))

"Kim, as you might imagine, we were not allowed to wander about the prison wherever we might want to go. We were escorted by the warden and made a professional appraisal of those parts of the factory to which we were taken."((CUT to Chairman Fielding interview in Capitol hallway))

"Today's Hearing was recessed and no vote was taken. Mr. Chairman, your committee took this bill under submission. What do you expect to do?"

"We intend to investigate the claims made today to see if indeed conditions are what we heard. If so, we will certainly take appropriate action."((CUT to Kim standing in front of Capitol))

"Prison industries are big business. Lagrimas is the largest of all, with over five million dollars in sales annually, all to the state of California. Seventy per cent of these sales come from factories that have never been checked or even seen by anyone outside the institution.

"We reached Warden Duane Clayborne this afternoon, who informed us that a full investigation would be made into how the finger was smuggled out of Lagrimas. When asked how many men had been maimed in the furniture factory during his 4-year administration, the Warden stated that he could not answer any questions until the results of his internal investigation were in. This is Kim Flint at the Capitol for Channel Two Eyewitness News."

Whoops and cries rang throughout the house.

"Aaron, what's next?"

"Don't know. We got documents showing Morris lost his finger last month, and other paper grenades to lob. Session ends in two weeks—we might jar something loose. Let's eat."

Blue sky faded to dusky rose as the sun went down behind the yard. Date palms transformed into silhouetted cut-outs as they lost their color and depth. The crowd ate and drank; noise and laughter increased as the lubricating effects of alcohol took hold, assisted by the mercifully quick cooling of the air that followed the setting of the sun. For exactly eleven minutes mosquitoes harassed everyone, and then disappeared. Two planets and a star replaced them. No one was inclined to go inside.

Art was ebullient. He rolled on with the easy, inexorable flow of a river, telling jailhouse war stories about failed capers, elaborate schemes of bank and credit card fraud that fell of their own weight, impulsive lunges for money that fell short.

"Didn't you ever get away with anything?" asked Robert.

"Man, I wasn't that bad a thief when I was at it for a living. Drugs tripped me up, no doubt about it, but I made a lot of money. Sooner or later, though, I'd get caught, and have to hock my boats and chinchilla coats and give all my money to lawyers and bail bondsmen. One day during my last turn through Folsom, it came to me that I wasn't really a free man like I'd always thought, workin' alone or with partners who I picked out myself. Truth was, I was working for the prison guards and and parole officers and probation officers and judges and sociologists"—Art flashed a quick look at Raphael—"that lived off of crime. I was nothin' but the raw material for a whole goddamned industry I was carrying on my back. It was too much weight, too heavy to carry, so I said the hell with 'em, and checked out.

"Nowadays, guys I used to know and steal with come around with big ideas and rolls of money, tellin' me lies about big scores and can't-miss schemes, and I always tell 'em to give the Union ten percent, because they're gonna need us sooner than they think."

Robert mulled Art's words over and thought, What *would* all those people do without criminals? How would they feed their families? The notion of cause and effect jiggled, then evaporated, leaving him with a queasy stomach. He put down his beer, and rose to go to the bathroom. The night was pitch black outside the small sphere of light defined by Aaron's lantern. The porchlight glowed in the distance. He stepped gingerly toward it as Teresa began telling of her first visit to Folsom prison as a student of Aaron's. She was still talking when he returned.

"Another guard came from God knew where and led me down a narrow hall between several more glassed-in offices holding people who could be seen but not heard, to a tiny room at the hall's end. The room was divided in half by glass, and had a counter, a chair, and a telephone on each side.

"He sat me down and locked me in, and I waited through another Ice Age until two guards escorted a prisoner down the same corridor and into the other half of the room and locked him in.

"He was a Chicano, about my height, compact body tattooed all over. He had three teardrops tattooed under his left eye that I had a very hard time not staring at.

"The only way to talk was over the phones. I said hello, and introduced myself. He said, 'Buenas tardes,' and something in Spanish to the effect that he couldn't speak English. Well, the truth is, I don't speak Spanish."

"What?"

"After our family moved from Del Rey to a smart new suburb of Fresno my father laid down the law—only English. 'I don' wanna raise no Speedy Gonzales cummedians,' he said. So, my visit was a big, big fiasco. After a minute of stumbling around, it became clear that I couldn't do what I was sent there to do. I saw the other clients and tried to leave. The guards sat thirty feet away. I knocked on the door to get their attention. One of them stared at me, but none of them stirred. I could feel the eyes of the last guy I talked to so I acted a bit restrained, but after twenty minutes of little knocks and holding my breath and waiting and no response I didn't care, and I banged as hard as I could on the door. Nothing!

"I started having visions of never getting out. Finally, just about when pure panic was about to carry me off, someone moseyed down the hall scratching his balls, and unlocked the door.

"If it had been just a crummy experience I might have let it all go, but that deliberate meanness . . . I could not *not* help Aaron so long as he had the nerve to sue them."

"Guards don't believe prisoners are active agents," said Raphael. "They're convinced there'd be no problems at all in prison if it weren't for 'outside agitators'. They believed it a hundred years ago when they were pissing and moaning about reporters. Now it's lawyers. They think like plantation owners who believed their slaves would've stayed happy forever if it weren't for the goddamned Abolitionists."

"What do those teardrops mean, anyway?" asked Robert.

Art yawned. "I dunno. One for every time he went to the pen, one for every man he killed. Maybe just that he had served time. Maybe it don't mean a thing other than that he wanted to see if he could stand to get three teardrops tattooed under his eye." He pulled his stiff, satisfied body up from the lawn chair. "It's been a long day. We've got to hit the road."

Ninety minutes later, the electric bus carrying Robert across San Francisco left the dark, quiet residential and warehouse district at the foot of the hill on which the Union building perched, and entered the Mission District. Stores were still open ("ropa para caballeros" . . . cowboy lassos? He resolved to learn some Spanish), people still in the street, mostly dark and some whites, long-haired men and short-haired women, at the Roxie Theatre or in Mexican restaurants; liquor stores, knots of people on the corners (the Usual Suspects, he remembered Raphael telling him, when Raphael had still been the man who wrote books students were required to read: "Cops don't sweat around with dangerous, tricky, expensive detective work like Kojack does on TV. They go down to the corner and round up the Usual Suspects."

The lights faded after their biggest splash at the corner of 16th Street and Mission, and Robert's bus moved through a neighborhood of interconnected residences, all the buildings three stories high with bay windows, no two exactly alike, shops on every corner. A half moon hovered just above the silhouette of the Mission Dolores, first enclave of Europe built on the thumb of land that became San Francisco. Robert tried to imagine the Mission's surroundings as they appeared in the late 18th century, but failed. The intricate density of the wooden houses, some with peaked roofs and some with flat roofs, their siding and trim and scalloped shingles and gimcrackery adornments painted innumerable faded colors, seemed as permanent as the sandstone cliffs behind the home he had left on the banks of the Ohio River.

The bus whooshed across Market Street and angled due north towards his apartment. As always, Robert became vigilant as the bus moved through the Fillmore District. "It used to *jump* before they tore it all down," Tyrone had told him, "but it's empty and mean over there now, nothin' but a bunch of housing projects. If I were a skinny little White boy like you, I'd stay on my toes."

The bus crossed Geary Boulevard and moved through Japantown and a prosperous neighborhood of stores, restaurants, and bars. It climbed a steep hill to the grand houses of Pacific Heights and a view of the yellow fog lights strung along the Golden Gate Bridge, the twinkling lighthouse on Alcatraz, and the dark mass of mountains across the mouth of the bay.

"Hey, Lee-roy, I think this must be your stop." Robert opened his eyes, shook his head, stood up and stumbled off the rear of the bus. The night was clear and cool. The tidy streets, gingerbread houses and geometric hedges in the small front yards of his neighborhood were so formal and carefully maintained that they seemed like a stylized recreation of human dwellings built for a museum of anthropology rather than for actual habitation. The effect was rarely sullied by people in the street.

Robert stood on the sidewalk in front of his apartment, staring and swaying. It was very easy, and pleasant, to lose a dimension in the even blue light of the many street lamps and see all the houses with their tiny turrets, arched windows, and trimmed foliage, as a painting on a long scroll, a backdrop waiting for events to take place in the foreground, or a screen blocking the view of tumultuous crankings and turnings behind, or as masses of colorless textured light and shadow creating the impression of emptiness here and bulk there. . . . he shivered and yawned, and returned to his slender, pale body. God, I'm the same color as these awful lights, he thought, scrutinizing his forearm. Got to get outdoors, get in the sun. He unlocked his side door, fell straight to bed, and dreamed of the hot wet summer days of his childhood that meant school was out and anything was possible.

7

TWO WEEKS LATER, THE LEGISLATURE PASSED A BILL THAT REPLACED the Civil Death Statute with the Civil Rights Statute—and also passed a bill allowing a modest amount of worker's compensation for prisoners injured on their jobs. The following day Art met with a newspaper reporter for lunch downtown. When he returned to the office he found a message asking him to call Dennis Mote, Chief Deputy Director of the Department of Corrections.

Mote had been the most receptive of the correctional officials with whom the Union had met; Art called him promptly. Mote asked him for a private meeting. He would not indicate why, but promised that it would "cover topics of considerable interest to us both." Intrigued, Art asked other Union members what they thought. Curiosity overran all objections, and he was urged on to Sacramento.

"Art! It's good to see you." Liz Braun extended her hand.

"Good to see you, Liz," said Art, and he meant it. He had been waiting over half an hour on a molded plastic chair by the receptionist's desk, staring into a windowless pit occupied by dozens of female typists and their equipment.

"I'm sorry you had to wait. Follow me back to Dennis' office." Liz Braun, Dennis Mote's personal secretary, made his phone calls, and had been the first to greet members of the Union on each of their visits to Correction's headquarters in Sacramento.

"Dennis' meeting ran longer than he hoped, and he's had to put out some fires," she said. "Something doing in Soledad." Liz included Art in the mysterious world of firemen with a knowing glance. "Have a seat; he'll be right out."

Art sat for another ten minutes by Liz's desk, this time in a cushioned chair. It was a large desk just to the left of a heavy wood door on a thinly populated edge of the central space. His keen anticipation and readiness for the meeting steadily eroded as he waited. Finally the door opened. Art stood promptly, and shook the outstretched hand of the man he had come to see.

"Good morning, Art! I'm glad you could make it. I've got to see the Director about something that can't wait. Go on in and make yourself comfortable."

When the door shut behind him the clatter of typewriters, telephones, and voices ceased. Art heard only the deep throb of a distant air conditioner blending with the hum of cool air forced through an over-head vent. A mantle of velvet dark descended, and Art was briefly unbalanced. When his eyes adjusted, he saw floor-to-ceiling curtains across the entire opposite wall, a gleaming dark wood desk to his left, and a pair of couches at perpendicular angles in the far corner some thirty feet distant, the only places to sit.

He crossed the office, his tentative footsteps completely muffled by the thick carpet. While Art sat in the quiet and puzzled over the absence of the normal office accoutrements—telephone, dictaphone, paper—the trappings of power, like viral hordes, drilled unseen through his cell walls and insinuated themselves in every part of him.

The door opened, and a brief flash of light and noise swept in along with the Chief Deputy Director. Art stood, and was waved down into his seat by Dennis Mote, who walked briskly across his office and sat on the opposite couch. Mote was a very tall man with a long face marked by strong vertical lines, a narrow nose, a furrowed forehead and corners of his mouth that dropped sharply down. He pressed a button atop a small black box on the table that separated the two couches. "Liz?"

"Yes?" Her voice spiralled out of the box and grated gently across Art's ear.

"Hold all my calls for a while."

"Right."

He turned to Art; his doleful mien was somehow comforting. "Art, I'll get right to the point. We've been very impressed by our meetings with the Union, particularly by their *tone*. It's been a real education for all of us. The Director said something after our last meeting that has stuck with me. He said, 'I've personally felt for quite a while that we've got to get out of our crisis reaction mode and try preventive action. Now might be the time.' "

Mote paused and added, in deliberate tones, "One of our real problems has been an inability to distinguish between those who disagree with us and those who are dangerous. We're learning. I hope you have also found our meetings productive."

"Yes we have." Art was surprised and pleased by this well-turned distinction, and made a mental note to remember and use it in the future.

"Well, we all kind of backed into meeting with each other, but this Director is interested in exploring ways and means to make them part of the system. Last week, he authorized me and our counsel, that's Kegley and Livingston, to work with you and your people in coming up with a mutually acceptable proposal for a pilot union of inmates in one of our prisons."

"Oh, yeah?"

"That's right. I know it won't be easy coming up with something both of us can live with, but it seems to me that its worth a try. We've worked so well together that I think the idea of institutionalizing our meetings—and having similar exchanges in every prison in the state—just might open channels of communication enough to stop some of our problems before they start."

Mote's broad smile shattered his facial harmony. "You know, I've been working for almost fifteen years to obtain formal recognition for bargaining units of state employees." He waited expectantly, and fell back into a more comfortable and impressive air of self-contained melancholy when Art did not respond. "I'd like to keep it quiet at this stage, and 'come out' only if we hammer out something we can all live with," he said. "Is it worth a try?"

"Well, I don't know. . . ." A cloud of excited thoughts buzzed like gnats in Art's brain. "Are you thinking of letting outside people meet inside as well?" he asked as casually as he could. "We'd have to have some kind of regular participation and check by people on the outside, to know what's really happening and make sure things are goin' like they should."

"Art, as far as I'm concerned, everything is up for grabs. I don't think we should set any preconditions or limitations."

Mote paused, and waited.

"I'll have to give it more thought, and run it by everybody else—the other people in the office—but if it don't work out I guess we haven't lost anything."

"My feelings exactly."

Art asked several more questions. Mote answered him with vague encouragement. After twenty minutes Mote looked at his watch. "I've got to go. We have a meeting scheduled with all the parole district supervisors." He stood, as did Art. The two walked across the office. As they reached the door, Mote hesitated, stopped and turned toward Art.

"You know, I have no illusions about the flak you'll catch if we go ahead, even if we give you a whole prison to run. I hope you know that the great majority of our staff will be initially dead set against our efforts, as they have been against every important reform of the last fifty years. Both of us will face considerable grumbling from our constituencies." Dennis Mote's head shook sadly as he spoke.

Art realized he was right, and said, "Hey, we're attacked every week for one reason or another. We know something about staying on course and answering back when we have to without getting too rattled."

"That's a good working definition of leadership, Art." The two men shook hands firmly, and abruptly pulled away, abashed by the warmth of their contact. Art moved quickly to fill the gap. "We're gonna meet tonight. I'll call you tomorrow, and we'll set up a timetable if we agree to go ahead."

"Sounds good. It would be nice to get together a proposal before our next quarterly meeting of all the wardens, but I'd rather have every brick in place than rush to meet any deadline." As Mote turned the doorknob, he added, "By the way, congratulations on getting the Civil Death Statute abolished. We've known for years that it was an anachronism, but its not the kind of thing we can take the lead on."

Art savored a slow drive back through the Delta between Sacramento and San Francisco. It hadn't occurred to him that his colleagues would react any way but favorably.

"Jesus, what a bunch of deadwood," he finally said in exasperation when none of his leads was picked up. "For years we've schemed on how to get Union meetings inside, and when we get the chance y'all are sittin' there like junkies on a stool."

"Man, it makes me nervous to rub up so close to those people," said Tyrone.

"Why? You're on a damned Mayor's Commission, always talking to bureaucrats about one thing or another."

"I'm tryin' to find jobs, talkin' on behalf of convicts. That's what we do, man. Let them run their own damned pens."

"Looking at it from the CDC point of view," said Raphael, "it would be very useful to have someone interposed between them and their charges—someone they could hand difficult problems to, someone they could blame. A lightning rod for resentments at a cheap price, as well as kudos for being progressive. I can see what's in it for them. What's in it for us?"

"Sounds like they want us to do their dirty work."

"Nothing will work if we pussyfoot around, that's for sure." Art came forward and pounded the table. "Listen! Our money's runnin' down, our stock is at an all-time high, we're getting flooded with mail—we've got 'em scared! Now's the time to negotiate! So they want us to catch shit that belongs to them, and so they want to head us off at the pass, so what? That's because we're *moving*. They didn't give a shit about us back when we were pure, but now they have to negotiate— We've hit 'em fair and square, everywhere!"

"Hooee! Scrape that boy off the ceiling! What kinda joy juice they servin' up in Sacramento!"

Art quieted down, but remained in dead earnest. "We don't have to agree to anything that doesn't look good to each and every one of us. If it works for a few months, we can get people in here from all over the world. There's not a goddamned thing happening in prisons these days. People are hungry for ideas. If we develop a model that works even a little, everybody will want to know about it."

"Could we do it at Lagrimas?" asked Teresa.

"I don't know. We could insist on Lagrimas, and have nothin' to do with some camp 500 miles away. There's plenty of good reasons to stop the process, and then go ahead on and shoot our shot in the courts. All

I propose is that we start it. Nobody else worth a damn will get the chance."

"How do we know the Director or anybody else besides Mote is really for this idea?"

"Details! If he's not, it's obviously all off. We can find out tomorrow. Here's my proposal: we set Teresa to draft a model proposal, after talking to each of us, and come up with something we all like. Then, we get together with the CDC. One step at a time. Let's vote on it, and I don't want anybody to vote for it unless they believe it has a chance of bein' great and they're ready to work to create it, defend it and carry it through. We have to all feel good about it or nothing we come up with will have a chance."

Art's proposal passed, without dissent or great enthusiasm. He called Dennis Mote the next day. "Dennis. Everybody thinks its worth a try."

"Good!"

"We're working on something right now. We'll need to meet with you all fairly soon to get an idea of whether we are anywhere near an agreement." Art cleared his throat. "We'd like the Director to be there, too, so we can get a sense of his thinking."

"I understand. He's a busy man, but I'll arrange a meeting with him and the other deputies, and three or four of your people. What's your schedule like?"

8

"QUARTER A LOOK AT THE INCREDIBLE STUB!" MORRIS YELLED ON THE day the news of his finger's progress hit Lagrimas. Abolition of the Civil Death Statute made Chilly's Dynamite Digit the pivot of the prison. The Fly was dying to hear a first-hand account. Finally, a letter from Teresa came scheduling a visit near the end of August, one year and a day after he first met her.

His days of slipping invisibly through the central corridor were gone; it was handslaps, glares, questions, jokes, smart remarks, requests for appointments, all the way to V-wing. Carruthers, Johnson and Magon were waiting in the anteroom when he arrived. Magon was gleeful. "Hey man, Robinson's on vacation. They're gonna let us in all at once."

Sure enough, they milled around naked for a minute, and were told to dress up and move out. Like an obedient herd heading for dinner, they crowded through the steel door and into the visiting room.

They walked through a narrow space between the backs of lawyers and girlfriends on telephones talking to men in glass boxes who were deemed too dangerous or disobedient to touch their visitors. As they entered the main room the Polaroid Master barked orders to a pair of lovers while other lovers and families waited patiently to be photographed. Surnames boomed over squawky speakers. Teresa was visible far across the room in her cubicle. She did not see them until they were very close.

"What happened?"

"A new guy saw we were all ducated for one person, so here we are."

"Well, this is a treat."

"Let's sit out with the peons," said Magon. They pushed together two formica-topped tables while a steady stream of quarters kept soft-drink cans banging down metal chutes behind him. "We think it was wonderful," said Magon gravely, "the way you guys gave everyone the finger."

Fred Johnson shook with laughter, and slapped his thigh. "That was all right, Teresa, you all put that together real nice. It's the hottest thing in the pen. Took the heat off of us, and put the spotlight *on*."

"Yup. We have become cynosures." The Fly pronounced the last word in an elongated, provocative way. Magon rose to the bait.

"What?"

"C-y-n-o-s-u-r-e." The Fly's voice rose above the slamming of steel doors and barred gates. "Look it up."

Nearby children waiting for their fathers played, fell, and cried. "I'm not sure what it means," said Carruthers, impatient with the old man's tricks, "but I am sure that now is the time to move ahead." Sounds ricocheted back and forth off concrete block walls; they all leaned forward. "The Union is very hot. Two administrators have approached me on their own and said they think the Union is the first good idea they've heard in a long time—even the old Guard that hates us can't come up with anything bad to say other than just throwing shit in the air."

"Well, feature this." Teresa pulled a handful of paper from a manila folder. "The Director of the prison system has asked us to come up with a proposal for a pilot program of a formal prisoner organization. I brought a tentative outline. Read it carefully, and let me know what you think. One point we'll insist on is that it happen here in Lagrimas."

She could hear wheels turning and gears meshing as they pored over her outline. Magon finally frowned. "What will this do to our lawsuit to get the right to meet?"

"If we don't reach an agreement, then we go ahead and sue."

"Not to change the subject," said Magon, "but try this one on. How about a name change? We're no longer civilly dead, right? So we're not a Union of the Civil Dead." A child on his left tripped over Magon's shoe, and began to bawl. Magon lifted him and jiggled the child on his knee. "This is the way the *farmers* ride," he sang.

"The law won't go into effect until January 1," Carruthers said absently as he pored over his copy of the 6-page proposal.

"So have a formal name change and a Resurrection party on New Years Day," Magon suggested. "Invite everybody." He pointed at his unopened copy of the proposal. "Does this give us the right to strike?"

"No."

"Strikes are no good in prison", Carruthers decreed. "We have no economic leverage over the people who run the prison—they work overtime and make *more* money if we strike."

"Hey bro, what's happening?" A young man dragging a barely dressed and heavily made-up companion walked up to Fred. "Y'all keep on keepin' on, you're doin' *great.*"

"Right on." Fred held out his hand.

"Come on, we'll lose our place in line." The young woman prevailed, and Fred turned back to the group.

"One-day strikes are another matter," Carruthers continued. "When they're co-ordinated with other prisons and focused on one issue, like hospital care, and announced by press releases, they're a good way of spreading the—"

"Teresa, you think these people are really serious?" Fred looked at her intently. Teresa smiled.

Magon held up his hand like a schoolboy who needed to pee. "Hey, let's step back for a minute," he said. "You know what? We might flop belly up on any day of this week or next. We might all get hurt or get sent off in five different directions, or . . . worse yet, we might succeed, and become stuffy dignitaries here in our own little puddle."

Protests came; Magon held up both palms. "Right now, though, nobody has got hit around here for months. The Union is growing strong. I suggest that we kick back for exactly one minute—" Magon looked at his watch—"and bask in the warm glow of our success."

Carruthers began to remonstrate against fatalism and existentialism. The Fly inhaled, intending to gloss on Magon's estimate of future outcomes. They each paused to let the other speak as their three companions leaned back in their chairs.

"All right, Serge." Carruthers spoke softly, and leaned back in his chair. So did the Fly. Magon's smile was irresistible. An oasis of well-being enveloped them in the midst of the loud, hot, stuffy jam-packed visiting room. They all smiled, and felt a surge of electrical current join them that felt so good no one wanted to speak and break the spell.

Of late, Magon seemed to be able to see down future channels as easily as he could see across the visiting room. Though his friends thought they were pausing to sniff the flowers on their way up the hill, he knew they had reached the peak. The Union's course would not be straight or smooth, but it would soon head down. Telling them about this would change nothing. Either he would not be believed, or he would persuade, and his injection of doubt would hasten the process of decline. All he could do was make sure that the peak did not pass unnoticed, to be dimly remembered only when they were tangled in thickets down below.

Teresa sped back to the Bay Area, but arrived an hour late for dinner with her son Guillermo, who was staying with her brother in Oakland. Later that night she drove Guillermo with her across the bridge over the bay to spend a rare weekend together at home.

The night was hot and still. She looked out her car window at the lights of San Francisco and their reflection in the unusually smooth metallic surface of the water below. As she turned off the freeway, she smelled the stench of diesel exhaust.

"Mom, I *itch*." Guillermo moaned and scratched himself.

A game with intricate, unspoken rules between the two of them had evolved since her son's miserable case of poison oak two years earlier. Guillermo would say that he itched; Teresa was to give him a thorough lotion massage without demanding that he produce any rash or other physical proof, but he could not assert his claims too often. "I'll rub you with ointment when we get home," she said.

Her third-floor apartment on the top of the Union building was stifling, hotter than it had ever been. She opened every window, dragged a mattress onto her narrow back deck, and began to rub. Her son slowly squirmed, his body turning and turning as if it were on an invisible spit. Yards, porches, gardens, clothes lines, and low fences rose beneath them up the hill, all contained in a bowl of humanity at ease, without the burden of display. An old man in underwear was visible in one of the lighted windows, laboriously pulling himself to his feet.

She rubbed and rubbed; the electric bus out front appeared and disappeared with roars that swelled and subsided like the pounding of long waves. Her fingers tightened, became numb, and her wrist muscles cramped.

Suddenly Guillermo sat up, his thin five-year-old body erect. "You're gonna quit now, aren't you?" he accused.

"I'm going to stay right here and rub you till you go to sleep, I promise." She rubbed the child slowly, methodically, from the tips of his feet to the top of his spine. He whimpered and turned, checking on occasion to see if his mother was flagging. Much later, his choppy breaths deepened and he lay still on his stomach, his eyelids fluttering. Teresa leaned down and whispered, "Do you feel better?"

He was asleep. His dusky skin was beautifully smooth, and covered with a fuzz faintly illuminated by the ambient dark orange light of the city. She remembered him as a tiny baby nursing at her breast with all his might, temples sweating as he sucked, and leaned down to give him a kiss. In the midst of wondering where to put him now that his mattress was on the back porch, Teresa also fell asleep. She found herself on the back porch when her eyelids were hammered by the bright morning sun.

9

THE DIRECTOR HIMSELF SAT THROUGH THE NEXT MEETING BETWEEN the Union and the Department of Corrections. He said nothing, and looked at the conference room walls when he was not studying his hands. The other administrators of his entourage scrutinized Art, Raphael, and Teresa with a devouring curiosity, as if they were examining new moles that had popped up overnight through the surface of their skin. No real discussion took place.

Union representatives drove to Sacramento twice that fall. The curiosity of the Deputy Directors became so strong that they agreed to schedule a meeting at the Union's San Francisco office. And so, one wet December Tuesday, the four administrators settled around the dining room table. After a perfunctory meeting, everyone went downstairs to the office.

"Ahhh, signs of life," sighed the Department's Assistant Counsel, his eyes glazed with nostalgia. "Very nice," murmured another as he examined the printing press in the corner. Two other officials withdrew far behind their blue serge shields. Dennis Mote stood by nodding slowly, like a man waiting for the verdict in a state fair sheep-judging contest next to an animal he knows is a real contender.

"What's next?" asked Raphael of Dennis Mote.

"I think we've done very well, well enough to truly say we have the skeleton of a workable idea. It's time to reach out. We're going to show this to some of our key people, and get back to you sometime after the beginning of the year."

IO

Every morning in January Art looked forward to the mailwoman's appearance. On days she was late he glanced up from whatever he was doing at any movement of the front doors. His anticipation built steadily until the middle of the month, when it became barely tolerable. He spent much of one Wednesday considering whether to call Dennis Mote in Sacramento. As he was on the verge of dialing, the telephone rang.

It was Bruce Cuniberti, a reporter for the afternoon paper. "Seen the final edition?" he asked.

"You know I don't read your rag unless we're in it."

"That's why I called you up. Take a look, and call me back. I'm at MacNamara's."

Art went down to the corner grocery. As he was about to push open the door, a panel truck pulled up in front with fresh newspapers. The headline read CALIFORNIA'S CONVICTS TO UNIONIZE? A tremor of dread coursed through him as he groped for change. Everyone in the office gathered around the story. It was an "exclusive" from Sacramento that hinted at a secret plot, a cabal of high officials working in tandem with ex-convicts. Officials of the guards' association were "appalled" to learn of such a plan, particularly since "we've had a helluva time getting them to recognize our union. Now, they want to give convicted criminals privileges denied to us. It's an outrage, and we're demanding that the Director be fired."

The phone rang. Art quickly reviewed with Rita Coburn what she would say to reporters, and went upstairs to call Cuniberti and Dennis Mote.

He could not reach Mote; he told Liz of the news story. "Oh, I'm afraid we know all about it," she told him. "Dennis will call you as soon as he can. He's with the Director right now."

Cuniberti's tone was consoling. "The guards have got their teeth in this one. I talked to the head of their association; he smells a win, and says they ain't gonna let up. The Governor's office had already denied any knowledge. Everybody's peeling off."

"What about the Director?"

"Nothing yet. He promises a statement before the end of the day. I'll call you when we get it."

Sometime near the end of a hectic afternoon Cuniberti called back. With Teresa taking notes on the other line, Art listened to him read the Director's press release. It began with fluff about how he was "continually searching for new ideas to lessen the level of tension and violence for staff and inmates", and stated that he had solicited a proposal from the Union "in order to provide for an exchange of information, increase mutual understanding, and lessen the number of lawsuits". The bottom line was, "We have determined that the potential threat to security posed by this proposal outweighs any speculative merits at this time." The Director concluded by stating that "The goals of the proposal could largely be achieved with less danger by the formation of Inmate Advisory Councils administered by local prison staff, without the involvement of outside persons who do not share the concerns of staff and inmates. Accordingly, I am today ordering that such councils be created in each facility."

"Fuckin' worthless company unions," Art muttered.

The phone rang again; it was Liz. "Art?"

"Yes."

"Dennis wants to talk to you. He'll be right with you."

Art waited a moment, and another.

"Hello, Art?"

"Yes."

"Have you seen the Director's statement?"

"Yeah."

"I'm terribly sorry. We sent the proposal out to all the Wardens. One of them must have given it to the guards' association. They've been unhappy with us since our affirmative action program began. It's been pretty grim around here."

Art was silent.

"You know, Art, sometimes if the leader gets too far out in front of his troops, he's all by himself." Art thought he heard a sniffle. "You just can't win a war that way. I feel very bad about the way things have gone, just awful."

"It's all right, Dennis," Art said automatically.

"Listen. If you or any of your people ever have any kind of problem, by God, don't hesitate to call. We won't tolerate any kind of harassment."

"Okay, thanks, Dennis."

"Working with you has been one of the best experiences I've had here." Mote was choked up.

"Take it easy. We tried; things don't always work out."

"Sometime when this all blows over, Art, I'd like to have a drink with you and talk about some of the unbelievable things we've run into up here."

"That'd be nice."

"Good luck, and tell everybody how sorry I am about the way things haven't worked out."

"I will."

"Good-bye."

"Bye."

II

IN THE MIDST OF DISAPPOINTMENT, TERESA TURNED TO THE CENTRAL task she had been hired to do—suing the state to gain the right of Union members inside prison to hold meetings. Unsure of how to do it, she rummaged through the entire Union archives from its founding in 1969, and haunted law libraries in San Francisco, Berkeley and Oakland. She read dozens of legal opinions from around the country, chased all their footnotes, and took home books about the history and shifting purposes of incarceration to read in bed.

The cyclic story of imprisonment gave her no reason to be sanguine about her project. From solitary confinement to the indeterminate sentence, the most oppressive features of prison life had been initiated by well-meaning reformers; but Teresa was never one to linger over the inevitably discouraging lessons of history. She never felt so alive as when she was entirely possessed, and from her immersion in the administrative regulations of confinement and biographies of celebrated convicts came a sweet sense of her own freedom.

While pacing one evening around the basement of the University of San Francisco law library between the bathroom and the snack machines, an architectural vision of the lawsuit came to her. The actual brick-and-mortar work of constructing it tilted her from exhilaration through distraction toward exhaustion. She slept little, and burned to finish it. By the end of March she was done.

Teresa drove to Lagrimas to obtain the signatures of her clients and to file the lawsuit in the Grapevine County Courthouse. As she sat in her prison cubicle awaiting her clients she relived the experience of watching their proposal for a Union inside unexpectedly evaporate. Art had been despondent since it fell apart.

How naive they had been to imagine that the support of a handful of top bigwigs could make something happen in a bureaucracy that drifted at glacial slowness in whatever direction it was already going regardless of what kind of directives were spewed out of its top! Well then, why would the words of a handful of judges make any difference? She was spared the need to follow this train of thought by a light tap on the glass. David Carruthers stood beaming with an infectious grin.

"Congratulations, Teresa!" They shook hands. "You guys did great." David bounced lightly as he spoke. "We've already had an Order posted saying that Inmate Advisory Council election procedures will be posted within ten days."

"But we lost! These 'councils' are so vulnerable, they can be disbanded on a minute's notice!"

"We're painting the whole thing as a victory. The Union took advantage of an opportunity it had created by its earlier work to make a proposal that was so solid that it boxed Corrections into a corner—they couldn't live with it for fear of a line staff rebellion, but they couldn't discard it—and their own efforts—as worthless. If Sacramento dropped the whole thing, they would look weak, plain and simple. So, the Union finally got us a council of elected prisoners that the Warden will have to meet with. He's already fucked up by saying six months ago that he didn't want one, that his staff was sensitive enough to what was happening that no 'new bureaucracy' was needed. Now, he's got to eat those words.

"So, we'll soon have an IAC. The only way to prove its limits is to use it up. We're gonna run for the IAC, and win. . . There's nobody else to vote for. I think we can even pick some quiet Union backers to be the 'disinterested' candidates. We'll pick our shots, and use this new podium to make points from. There are plenty of issues in here, a lot to talk about. Chances are pretty good that our warden will destroy and martyrize it before it sinks back into the soup of general indifference.

"If we push it to that point, our lawsuit will have more breathing room. They'll have to acknowledge that the IAC is not a reasonable alternative if their warden has destroyed it in two minutes one morning because he was tired of it getting in his face.

"Meanwhile, have you checked the latest statistics on stickings? Do you know there has not been anybody hurt in here for nine months? Over five thousand mad dog males, terrors of the civilized world. Pretty good, eh? We're making a hell of a record to talk about in court. Everything's falling into place."

Teresa thought she could hear his heart pound like a power plant running flat out. Victory or defeat? Half full or half empty? Although it didn't feel like a victory, there was no logical imperative in either direction. . . . Carruthers waited for what he deemed a decent interval, and said, "I think our best play is the diabetics."

"Huh?"

He then explained the situation of diabetics in Lagrimas state prison. Like other invalids, they were transferred to the central prison hospital only if they turned bright purple or made noises like a water buffalo. Otherwise, their treatment was simple. Upon initial diagnosis, an appropriate amount of insulin was set. Thereafter, each morning, no matter what, they received with that amount. However, their occupations, opportunities to exercise, and breakfasts changed constantly.

The results were frequent instances of excessive blood sugar caused by strenuous work after consumption of large globs of potatoes, bread and candy that resulted in irritable lethargy and vomiting (and disciplinary lockup for "drunkenness") or acidosis and coma.

On the other hand, whenever the prison was locked down, prisoners were confined to their cells without breakfast. With no food or exercise, insulin shock and unconsciousness followed the daily shot. None of the regular staff had received any training in the problems of diabetics.

The Lagrimas hospital, like most institutions created for the poor or confined, assumed that its patients malingered in order to "take advantage." It was designed to thwart and harass the indolent rather than heal the sick, and this it did well. Complaints both by the diabetics and by the prisoners who worked at the hospital went unheeded.

"It's a super issue," Carruthers concluded. "I think if we set it up right, we either clear it up for a quick win, or its worth a one-day strike."

When the Fly arrived for his visit with Teresa, she was sitting in her chair shaking her head. "I dragged in here today to tell you all the details about our failure, but now I'm almost ready to buy a bottle of champagne and celebrate our mighty victory."

"It's Carruthers," said the Fly. "The boy is a phenomenon. He looks like he belongs on the back of a Wheaties box, and thinks like Vladimir Lenin on a good day. I pitch in here and there, but mainly ride along with him and Fred Johnson. They're the local geniuses."

She gave him his copy of the lawsuit. He marvelled at its bulk. "They'll throw me in the Hole for possessing a dangerous weapon when they see the size of this. Man, it must weigh two pounds."

"Two pounds and two ounces, to be exact."

They reviewed the petition and talked of the dangers and possibilities of an informational strike centered on the treatment of diabetics. The Fly, Magon and Johnson all backed the idea.

At 2:30, when the visiting room closed for the day, Teresa was gently pummelled by a crowd of women and children as they all squeezed through the wing's narrow entrance gate. She filed the lawsuit at the Grapevine courthouse and learned that if the petition required the five days of court time for which she was asking, her case would not be heard until July.

While driving home, she saw that the hills around had reached their springtime pitch of intense emerald green, and decided that Carruthers was right. Wins and losses were subjective things outside of ball fields, susceptible to creation by faith, by doubt, by self-fulfilling prophecies.

"It won't work."

Teresa was stung by Art's quick response and his stubbornly protruding lower lip. "Why not?"

"Too risky. Strikes never work in prison. Our Folsom strike made a stir, but all it really did was fatten up some guards with overtime bonuses and get the warden a promotion."

"I think it's brilliant." Myrna leaned forward on the long table and brushed imaginary hair away from her face. "Action on behalf of diabetics will be a lot easier to sell than anything for prisoners."

"Diabetics?" Art was incredulous. "Why the fuck are we going to strike over diabetics? Have the diabetics sent us a petition, or what?" Art turned to Teresa.

"Well. . ."

"You don't know how we came to do diabetics, you just think it's a good idea."

"Do you think it's a bad idea?"

"I think Carruthers squeezed and poked and pinched around and finally picked out diabetics like an old woman picking out mangoes in a market. Something *bothers* me about that dude."

"Do you think it's a bad idea?" Teresa insisted.

"Hell, I can't say anything bad about helping diabetics, but we can figure out something better than a strike."

They wrangled interminably that evening over whether to support a one-day strike to publicize a proposal to end maltreatment of diabetics should the Inmate Advisory Council be ignored. Art was against it; Teresa and Myrna were for it; Raphael and Tyrone talked of whatever strike ramifications occurred to them; Robert said little.

Three hours later a consensus was reached to do it, but everyone was exhausted. Robert was very glad the two people who had agreed to volunteer that afternoon had not shown up to the meeting. He went against the current of depleted spirits around him, and spoke of overdue newspaper assignments and the need to reply to several opportunities, requests, and invitations in the mail.

"Next week, Robert," sighed Myrna. It was 11:30. "It'll be first on the agenda instead of last. Let's quit."

12

THE "INMATE ADVISORY COUNCIL" ELECTIONS UNWOUND AS THEY WERE meant to. I can die easy now, thought the Fly, and probably should; I've become and elected official. The Council met on the first Monday of March. The first item on the agenda was medical treatment. All members agreed to appoint Carruthers to survey the medical care at Lagrimas, and instructed him to report at the next monthly meeting.

Carruthers devised a plan that was endorsed by every diabetic he could lay his hands on. On a fine April Monday, he reported, at length and in considerable detail, and made a proposal that diabetics be housed together with a trained nurse who knew something about the pancreas. He concluded with, "In view of the importance of our proposal to the health of certain of our brothers, and the discrete nature of the problem, we ask for a response by the next monthly meeting."

Later on, certain officials complained that they were sucker-punched because the issue wasn't "really emphasized." What they meant was that no one told them that the convicts would do something if the staff did nothing. Halfway through the May meeting, the third and last, Fred Johnson stood and asked the Program Administrator for the administration's response to the proposal. The Program Administrator who sat in on the meetings said that the matter was still being looked into.

The next day 90 percent of the prisoner population did not appear for work. Press releases distributed by the Union the night before announced that the prisoners of Lagrimas would engage in a one-day work stoppage in support of their brothers suffering from diabetes.

Hospital workers and cooks were the only prisoners on the job. The cooks were sent back to their cells, and the administration declared the entire prison locked down, with everyone confined to their cells until further notice. No mail was delivered and no visitors were allowed, but many prisoners had radios that were tuned to every receivable wavelength. Lagrimas made four afternoon news reports. Three mentioned only that the convicts were on strike, and quoted the warden as saying he would do whatever was necessary, but one mentioned the maltreatment of diabetics and the fact that the work stoppage was for one day only. Cheers reverberated through the wings.

The prison came to a stumbling halt. All real work, transportation and distribution of goods, building maintenance, clerical work, communications, etc., was done by convicts. They ate baloney on stale bread twice a day and sat in their cells drifting, reading, gaming, yelling, and talking on the toilet telephone via the pipes.

The Fly stayed close to his radio. The story persisted. Coverage, to his amazement, was not entirely negative. Prison strikes usually fizzle out in a flurry of mutual recriminations under pressure of idleness, bad food, and the indifferent hostility of the public. The press, guided always by the friendly familiar Flak, the bureaucrat in charge of penitentiary P.R., focuses on the most trivial prisoner demands and makes no mention of the grievances that are central, while playing up the rap sheets of strike "leaders," that is, persons selected by the Flak to represent the strikers on the basis of the grossness of their rap sheet. It's a standard formula.

Not this time. The Fly heard two doctors discuss the nature of diabetes and describe what passed for current effective treatment. A diabetic who had been locked up in Lagrimas told of his experiences, and described the coma and death of one Leonard Teagle. The Flak in Sacramento stated that the Director knew little about the present situation but knew that Lagrimas hospital "had taken steps toward accreditation."

That opened a whole new can of worms. Nobody had known—or cared—that the hospital was not accredited. Few understood what non-accreditation meant, but it raised specters of moldy cadavers in corners and that great American horror: test-flunking. Nobody believed the prison's protestations that it didn't really matter.

The press tried to get inside and talk to members of the Council or diabetic prisoners, without success. The Warden cited "disruptive, volatile conditions" as his reason. He jumped around when answering questions about the treatment of diabetics, saying one day that no problems existed, and the next that problems were "being thoroughly reviewed." Art Simpson was heard on a Berkeley radio station demanding that a commission of outside doctors be formed to study and recommend, and that reporters be allowed access "immediately" to Lagrimas. "We don't know *what's* going on in there," he added darkly. Cheers sounded throughout the wing, and mingled with cries of "baloney on white bread, that's what's happening!" The Fly felt the calm gathering strength of the Buddhist who "just sits," and in that refusal to ebb and flow, gains higher ground.

He prepared as best he could for a "search and destroy" raid, a confiscation of radios or at least the dismantling of the elaborate antennae that had crept up cell walls shortly after radios had entered. Instead, Officer Weil came by after eight days and handed him a blurry ditto sheet stating that in view of the "restoration of normal conditions," all prisoners would be expected back to work the following day.

The impounded mail and newspapers came the next morning. Teresa came, bearing with her a ream of clippings from newspapers around the state detailing the course of events from start to finish. The last document was a press release from the warden saying that pending the completion of a "thorough review by the Superintendent of Prison Health," diabetics at Lagrimas would be transferred from their various quarters to one unit and placed under the care of a trained nurse. The core of the Council's proposal was achieved.

The Fly could scarcely contain himself. Strength veered into giddiness. "This is wonderful, absolutely without precedent. You all were great! How the Hell did you find the diabetic? We weren't close to breaking . . ." He babbled on, and noticed shortly that Teresa was not her usual self. She seemed flat and drawn.

"What's the matter?" he asked.

She hesitated. "Things aren't going very well at the office," she said, and lowered her head as if ashamed. He asked no more questions.

In May, right on the heels of the strike, a notice was posted on every bulletin board that the first stop of the Director's Statewide Tour would be Lagrimas on June 10–12, 1976. Nothing frightened staff so much as these visits from on high, when Sacramento ceased to be a powerful but comfortably remote abstraction akin to God, and materialized in the form of a real person, a King surrounded by arrogant, nosey lackeys. This time, there was only four weeks' notice.

Everything—glass, steel, concrete, wood, plastic and flesh—was polished and polished again. Leaky pipes, broken air conditioners, the inevitable attrition of a huge building subject to wide cycles of wet and dry, hot and cold, was frantically confronted when discovered—mind you, not systematically approached, but if a staff member noticed a leaky shower head he stood screaming and sweating until it was fixed.

The Yard was perfectly flat-topped, grass seed thrown on bare spots, flowers planted, files inspected and perfected. Obligatory entries not made in months were made late at night by staff members and by convicts who were promised the moon for cooperation. Opportunities for strategically placed prisoners to enrich themselves abounded, but for the most part, it was a time of hard and long work overseen by a horde of nervous wrecks.

Don Schulman, the Fly's current Education and Library Supervisor, was a retired military man who was not quite jovial or earnest enough to sell insurance. The Fly regarded him as a decent guy, considering the alternatives. Schulman came by one day late in May, a little bit brisker than usual.

"Fly, I want this library spitshined from top to bottom!"

"Don, I've got a legal obligation to keep the library running, and I'm giving legal assistance to several people." The Fly inhaled a breath of the haughtiest air he could find, and stated, "A visit from the Director isn't good cause to cut off *constitutionally* required services." Schulman flinched. The Fly played his hand as best he could, and Schulman finally promised to dig up a couple of laborers if the Fly would make sure the work was done.

During these preparations the medical committee recommended more extensive changes in the treatment of diabetics than were originally proposed. The prison accepted the recommendations, and ordered that they be implemented within 30 days. Staff was feeling beat down, and the Union organizers did their best to calm them. When Council members were separately told that Council meetings were "suspended," no one made a peep of an objection. "Give 'em a minute to digest," said Magon. "There's time enough to complain."

The application of soap, paint, and wax to their material surroundings climaxed in an orgiastic frenzy of rubbing and buffing that lasted late into the night before the King's arrival. Random cell searches turned up missing lawbooks as well as the usual assortment of blades and bottles of fermented foodstuff. The searchers also gave the Fly forty other confiscated lawbooks that were not part of the library, and he spent much time getting them back to their proper owners. Nine of them remained on his shelves, part payment for the "borrowed" volumes that he had lost.

Very late the night before His arrival, and thanks to a special "emergency" dispensation, the Fly sat at his oak desk trying to make out a new bit of graffiti revealed by the scouring of the top. The dark patina was gone, replaced by pale, wounded wood. About the time he determined that the rounded indentation spelled out "Fuck this place," Sergeant Huff lumbered up.

"Whose face did you get into," said the Fly, "to get stuck on the midnight shift?"

"It's only till July, thank God," Huff wheezed and sighed. "Better now when it's hot in the day than in the winter." He pulled up a chair, and sat across the desk. Their heads were at the same altitude.

"Say, Fly, listen up for a minute." Huff was quite serious. "The people upstairs really don't want anything to go wrong while the Director's here. They know you got juice, and they really want to get along better. If things go okay over the next couple days, they told me to tell you you can have almost anything you want."

"Who is 'you'? Me personally?"

"The Union people, the ones that woman lawyer always sees."

"What does 'things go okay' mean?"

"You can figure it out."

"Too fuzzy," insisted the Fly. "Get more specific, and maybe we'll talk."

Huff looked him straight in the eye. "Tell me what you really want, Fly, and drop this Union bullshit."

"The Union hasn't done one wrong thing and you know it," snapped the Fly. "It lives off of your fuckups. You already trashed the Inmate Advisory Council. What the Hell else do you want?"

Suddenly mindful of the "go-easy" policy, he said, "I'll think about it, and talk with the others. Nothing's on for tomorrow anyway. Hey, take it easy. We're about 72 hours shy of that great day in the morning after, when everything is clean and there's no awful visit on the horizon for years to come. You can do three days standing on your head in the shitter."

Huff involuntarily smiled, stood up, and left the Fly alone with his books.

The Director addressed a groggy population over the P.A. on the first day of his tour. He said there would be an "open meeting" in the gymnasium/auditorium on the third and final day, at which time he would be available to answer questions and hear comments—"praise or complaints." He also promised that he would not tolerate any retaliation.

The Director truly meant well, but he was out of touch. He could promulgate edicts by the bushel, but he didn't live or work at Lagrimas, and he didn't have the keys or the clubs in his hand. Everyone at Lagrimas, staff and convicts, had a firm grasp of that basic fact, and thought a little less of him for saying he would do what he clearly could not.

The Fly met with Fred, David and Sergio in the lunchroom after the encounter with Huff. Various officials had approached each one, and made more specific offers.

"Man, they tellin' me the Brotherhood can have the world on a platter, everything we been yearnin' for for the past ten years. We'd be in better shape than the Catholics! The shit is truly gettin' deep."

Sergio's eyebrows arched. "Deaver told me he could get me into an outdoor camp in the foothills behind Grapevine, and out on the streets in six months."

"Burroughs said they'll stick me in a work furlough halfway house in San Francisco if I keep my mouth shut for a week," said Carruthers. "I said, 'What if I get a job with the Union?' and he said, 'That's not my department.' " Carruthers shook his head. "I think they're gonna move me no matter *what* I do." Gnawing his thumbnail, he looked like a man pressed for time.

There was a brief cause while they all shoveled down food. They had around nine minutes to drink, talk, and eat. Magon suddenly looked up from his mashed potatoes, a fork in one hand, a spoon in the other.

"Man, it's the same old shit," he said. "In Mexico for 150 years now, you get together a big enough bunch of guys and shoot enough people, somebody will point at you and say 'Okay, you're on the team,' and make you a General. That story is too old, too tired. Here, check this out." He pulled a battered copy of the Union's latest paper from his pocket. " 'The Union confronts rather than circumvents rules it disagrees with.' I like that. It keeps me going. I ain't goin' for no deal—unless, of course," his eyes twinkled, "they offer me a million dollars. I can be bought, but not for no chump change."

No one spoke. They all returned to stuffing down food. Fred scooped up and swallowed the last of his potatoes, and said, "Okay, General, you call it," as the bell rang. They all went back to work.

Tickets to see the Director went fast. The Fly arrived early in the morning, but there were only a handful of scattered empty folding chairs on the entire basketball court. The sun's heat was reinforced by a thousand sweaty bodies. In spite of the formality of the occasion, everybody wore t-shirts, many emblazoned with the Union's logo, or tank-tops. By the time the show started, convicts lined the walls. The air was heavy with male sweat.

The Warden spoke first. He welcomed the Director, and introduced him and three top toadies. All five of them sat near the edge of the stage. The Director took the podium, and complimented everyone on the penitentiary's appearance, "for I know that in a time of great budgetary restrictions without your labor and cooperation it would not be possible to maintain the institution in such a high quality manner." He then complimented the Warden and his staff for their "stewardship" that had led Lagrimas to a period of an "unprecedented absence of violent incidents."

"And now," said the Director, "I want to leave as much time as possible to hear directly from you men. My staff is prepared to write down and will follow up on the points made. Please give your name and number before you speak, so that we may be able to reach you later, and follow up however necessary on your comments."

The Fly's hand went up along with about a dozen others, including Magon's. Since he looked like a harmless old crank of a Honkie, he was called on right away. He complained about the fact that the library had been gutted in order to make room for an expansion of the law library. After a plea that the Director order the library restored and a promise to describe how it could be done without building any new buildings, he sat down.

The Director promised that he would do what he could, but added that he could make no promises that he could do anything at all in light of the fact that his budget request had been "slashed" by the legislature. "Bullshit," murmured the Fly, loud enough to draw appreciative noises from those immediately around him.

The next few speakers either groused about the food or claimed that a great mistake or injustice had been made when they were sent to prison. Magon's hand stayed high, but he was overlooked as more and more prisoners were emboldened once they heard how foolish or ordinary their brothers sounded. His was one of fifty hands in the air with five minutes to go when the Director called on him to speak. His voice was loud and clear, easy to make out all over the auditorium. "Sir," he said, "I urge you to reconsider your decision not to allow a Chapter of the Union of the Civil Dead, now known as the Union of the Imprisoned since our civil rights have been restored, to be established in Lagrimas." Audible shuffling and buzzing and a couple of shouts arose. Magon summarized the benefits that would flow to both staff and convicts from such a step, and waited for the Director's reply.

The Warden sat still, with only the fists clenched in his lap speaking for him. The Director smiled complacently. With less than three minutes remaining, he was ready to answer the tough question.

"As you may know, we have given that proposal serious thought. There is much in what you say. We've talked to people all over the country, and considered a detailed proposal from the group that you mentioned. I do not intend to just let things drift while I am Director, and will continue to consider ways of increasing security and making 'rehabilitation' a reality instead of a hope." He paused and shifted his weight from one foot to the other while the Fly quelled a wave of nausea.

"Our review persuaded us that there were considerable risks and potential danger as well as benefits in a program wrapped up with people outside the prison who really can't share the concerns of those of us inside." The Director cleared his throat. "These concerns," he continued, "led us to reject the most extreme proposals in favor of Inmate Advisory Councils. These councils are a major building block in our plan to revitalize and modernize prison administration in California, and thrust California's prisons to the forefront again by making them responsive to a changing world." He concluded with, "I learned from the newspaper reporters calling about your hospital that the Lagrimas Council is an especially active chapter."

A ripple of laughter moved across the auditorium. The Director turned to a toady to see if he had to answer any questions and turned his eyes back to Magon, who remained standing near the edge of the auditorium halfway back from the stage. Everyone recognized the cue that Magon should sit down now, his moment past. But things didn't work out that way. He kept standing and reached toward the Director.

Magon sang out: "Sir, it is too bad that I have to be the one to tell you, but we no longer have an Inmate Council at Lagrimas." An anxious hum sounded, and the Director turned to look directly at Magon. "Our chapter was abolished after our third meeting, probably because of our work on behalf of diabetics, but we don't really know, because no reason was ever given. So, the shaky position of such a council is my last, best reason for urging that you think twice about it, and allow an organization that's got more staying power than some council that's got no outside connections, that the Warden can do in anytime he likes, for good reason, or bad reason, or no reason at all."

Magon then sat down. The Director looked at his boys. Their faces were blank. He then looked at the Warden, who looked at the floor.

"I thank you very much for your comments," he said grimly, "and for being interested enough in your prison to come today."

A few stood and applauded. They were rapidly followed by the rest, peasants turning to the King for respite from the nobles. The Director nodded once and left the stage.

Magon moved out of the hall in the midst of a knot of milling convicts. "All right, move it!" yelled a guard. The Fly maneuvered through the crush, and abruptly found him just outside the big swinging doors of the gym.

"That was fabulous," said the Fly, "but Jesus, I think you'd better be careful for a while. What happened to our plan to lie low?"

Magon managed to look both sheepish and radiant. "I planned on making the Union pitch, but the stuff about the Council being cancelled just popped out." The crush of people wanting to talk to Magon, or just see him, was intense. Milling convicts drove the Fly past and on down the hall.

That night he wrote in his journal, "There are whoops and whispers sounding around me tonight, and the air crackles with expectancy. It's a dangerous, habit-forming feeling I'm feeling, one of exposed nakedness in contrast to the usual folds of resignation that surround everyone—or me, at least—in here. I like it, I really do."

13

CARRUTHERS SAW THE CHIEF DEPUTY WARDEN IN THE HALL AFTER THE
Director's appearance, and asked him when the Warden's office would
answer the appeal seeking re-instatement of the Inmate Advisory
Council.

"It's past due, you know."

"That may have been one of the ones we misplaced."

"What?"

"I'm not sure, but why don't you file it again? Send me a copy this
time, and—"

"Shit!" Carruthers wheeled and went straight to the education office.
He re-typed the appeal and returned to the central corridor. The main
road of Lagrimas was jammed with staff and prisoners drifting with the
crowd or pushing against it with the practiced skill of Manhattanites
moving up an Avenue during rush hour.

The unmistakable bullet shape of the Warden's head loomed on the
other side of the corridor, coming toward Carruthers. When the Warden
drew even, his head determinedly fixed in a direction toward the opposite
wall, Carruthers pulled the proposal from his folder and shouted, "Warden!"

Everyone within range turned except the Warden; his answer was an
accelerated step forward. Carruthers turned and followed as fast as he
could, waving the appeal. "Warden! I have something for you!"

The Warden reached a patch of open field, and broke into a trot.

Carruthers picked up the pace. The Warden glanced back just as he reached his destination—the door to the Administrative Wing—and tried to stop, but his momentum carried him forward and he fell near the door with a crashing thud that froze everyone around at a respectful distance wondering whether it would be best to help the Warden up (he was a very large man) or pretend they did not see his fall.

Everyone, that is, but Carruthers. He broke through the circle and approached the Warden. "May I help you up, Sir?" He extended a hand.

"No!" bellowed the Warden.

Carruthers ignored the Warden's reply. "Here is our appeal, sir, that I gave to the Program Administrator, but has been lost. I want to deliver it personally." He held it out toward the Warden, and when it was not taken, dropped it gently on his body and stepped back into the crowd.

"Get out of my life!" the Warden cried, to no one in particular. The Warden clambered to his feet, gasping for air. His face was flushed. All else was frozen still. Two guards and a lieutenant sprang forward to help, but he waved them off impatiently and jerked open the steel-plated door to his wing like it was a screen door to a summer porch. "Why the hell do I still have to put up with this kind of shit?" he rasped under his breath. His question hung in the air as he walked through to safe territory and shut the door. Carruthers' appeal lay alone on the polished floor, shunned like a piece of radium that would sterilize anyone who touched it.

14

WHEN THE PHONE RANG, ART AND MYRNA WERE EATING SUPPER IN bed watching the evening news. Myrna answered. "Oh hello, Dennis, how are you?"

Art sat straight up, remembering his last encounter with the chief deputy director.

"Sure, he's right here." Myrna said, "It's Dennis Mote," and handed Art the telephone.

"Dennis! How are you?"

"Fine, Art, just fine. Sorry to bother you at such a late hour."

"No problem at all."

"Art, I understand that you all have a hearing scheduled in about three weeks, around July 6, on a lawsuit to obtain Union meetings inside Lagrimas."

"Yup. You and I are both going to testify."

"I know, I got my subpena last week. What's the goal of the litigation, Art, basically to bring about what we tried to do last winter?"

"Right."

A pause at the other end of the line extended long enough for Art to wonder if they had been disconnected. "Art, I don't think we're in the business of telling you what to do anymore than you are to tell us what to do. I'm not gonna ask you any questions about witnesses or anything else. That's your business. You know I want you to succeed, that I've gone a long way down the road to make it happen. All I want to do now is give you the benefit of my best judgment. What I want to say is confidential. I guess I need to add that if you cannot in good conscience keep it entirely to yourself, please tell me, and I won't burden you with it."

Art spoke too quickly. "Sure, Dennis, I can hold my mud. Whatever you say will stay right here with me."

According to Dennis Mote, the Warden at Lagrimas had been marked as a progressive comer within the system, a man willing to go with the new thrust of minority hiring but who still retained the support of the Old Guard—a man likely to move up to Sacramento and—who knows?—perhaps succeed the Director.

But, "the finger business and the thing with the diabetics have put Lagrimas in a bad light. They weren't well-handled, Art—they weren't contained at the local level. We've had some pretty unpleasant phone calls up here, including one from the Governor's office." The Director was personally affronted by the unilateral cancellation of his Inmate Advisory Council, and embarrassed to learn of it in a public forum through the mouth of a prisoner. The Warden's star was tarnished, falling, and he knew it.

"Art, the bottom line is, I don't know who's going to be in charge there in six months. Right now, the Warden is a desperate man. In six months, he'll either regain his perspective and recover lost ground—we're still willing to work with him—or he'll be out, replaced by someone who can take a lawsuit in stride. In either event, it seems to me you're liable to come up with a better result if you wait."

Art's head was spinning as the Chief Deputy Director concluded: "I know you'll do whatever you think best; I wanted to share with you what seems to me to be valuable information."

"What's up?" Myrna demanded as he hung up the phone. As always, Art told her everything.

"And was that the big secret you aren't supposed to tell anybody?"
He nodded.

"How do you suppose you'll handle that at the meeting tomorrow night? Are you not gonna tell anyone? Do you know how it will go over if you say, let's wait six months, and when people ask Why, you say, Sorry, it's confidential? And what do you want to do anyway? Wait six months or not?"

"Wait a minute," Art protested. "I just got the phone call. Gimme a minute to think."

"We're awfully low on money, honey. Plus we've got some good members in Lagrimas right now." Myrna was uneasy.

"Hell, haven't we said that a legal victory in this lawsuit is the surest way to get more grants, more members, more money?" The thought of proceeding without the Union's well-known Lagrimas prisoners wasn't altogether unattractive. "Mote as much as promised us a better deal."

Art Simpson, like most people, believed in the magical efficacy of inside information. As he pondered and mulled over the best course of action, his memory had already transformed Dennis Mote's possibilities of future change into inevitabilities. He expected his revelation, surrounded by the aura of an oath of secrecy, to have a profound effect on everyone present; and so it did.

Raphael had flown away to attend a distant conference, but all the other members of the Union sat in place around the dining room table for Wednesday night's meeting.

Art dove straight in. His demeanor was grave as he emphasized how necessary it was to win the lawsuit and swore everyone to secrecy before relating the contents of the phone call. He concluded with a suggestion that they seek a continuance until December. "They love delays on those civil calendars—shouldn't be hard to get at all."

"Ahh, man, I don't know, six months is a long time."

Tyrone shifted positions. He looked uncomfortable, as if he had swallowed a cockroach.

"Myrna, how much money does the Union have as of this minute?" Teresa asked.

"I don't know exactly, but it's something like twelve thousand dollars for sure, with five thousand maybe from the Franciscan Community."

"And how long can we last at our present rate of expenditure on twelve thousand?" Teresa yanked her voice back from its course upward. The room's atmosphere thickened with tension.

"Well, about five months, six if we give up lunch."

Myrna's effort toward levity fell straight to the floor.

Teresa turned to Art. "In August, two months from now, I will have been here two years, living on a pittance, away from my children. I don't mean to snivel, it's been *fine*, and will be fine so long as we are moving, but I will not sit on my hands for six months waiting for some miraculous bureaucratic gift. The lawsuit is all prepared. Subpoenas are out. We've got wonderful witnesses inside Lagrimas who could be moved any day. You and Raphael will be wonderful, and Dennis Mote will have his chance to be wonderful. In six months, I'll be gone, our witnesses will be gone, you'll be looking for something to do, and there won't *be* any lawsuit."

Art stared at Teresa. His agitated face jumbled in several directions, seeking in vain a unified expression. Teresa's voice continued rising. She was oblivious to all save Art.

"Have you considered that Mote may have been put up to call you, or volunteered to call to get back in the good graces of the people he works for? He isn't paid by us, you know. 'Hey,' " (Teresa dropped her voice an octave, in imitation of Dennis Mote), " 'I can call Art Simpson, mumble some bullshit, get the whole thing put off 'til Christmas.' Has it occurred to you that Mote might not be Mr. Nice Guy? That he might have other motives for the load of crap he laid on you over the phone? Remember the Director's reason he put out in his press release for dealing with us? To *avoid lawsuits.* I was hired to bring lawsuits. You told me around a campfire two years ago that bringing this very lawsuit was the reason I was hired, that you couldn't find anyone else with the gumption to do it."

Tyrone, Myrna, and Rita tried to speak at once, but Art had found his voice and overrode them all. "Goddamn it," he yelled, "I wanted you to sue the CDC, not take over the Union and carry it off! All we've been doing lately is doing what you tell us to do, or doing what you've been told to do by your honeys in the penitentiary, with you puttin' the legal gloss on it all. We've become the damned grunts in this army! Everything's done to help the lawsuit, or not done because it'll hurt the lawsuit. If what we do is set strictly by what we can sell in the courtroom, we've already lost everything."

"Sounds good, Art, sounds righteous. But what about the strike that you wanted no part of?" Teresa's voice steamed through her clenched teeth like a vapor. "You ought to look at yourself. I used to think your mocking of convicts was refreshing, realistic, but I'm beginning to think you don't like any part of them. You want to put convicts totally behind you, or be a parole officer and boss them around and trade stories about your naughty charges with other parole officers over drinks. Just because you weren't a sellout last year or the year before that does not guarantee you a lifetime of integrity."

Art started forward toward her, and sat back. His face turned brighter and brighter red until Robert was afraid it would explode like a spring bud and burst into bloom, a bloodred flower. Art yearned to rub Teresa out. She looked straight at him, contemptuous, indifferent to her fate. Art stood up abruptly, and fled the room.

"Art mighta come off with some sexis' bullshit, but that was kinda heavy, Terry." Tyrone looked even more uncomfortable, almost seasick. Robert was in a state of shock. Myrna rose from a grim exhaustion and said, "Terry, you're right, we got to go ahead, but there's ways of being so fuckin' right that you're wrong, dead wrong, and you just found one."

Teresa apologized weakly as Myrna left the room; she was drained. The meeting had finished.

15

Lieutenant Victor Sanchez walked through the main corridor of Lagrimas one morning late in June with pep in his step. He traded "Hello's", "Good morning's", and jibes like "workin' hard?"—"Hardly workin'!" whenever possible with the dozens of employees going home after the midnight shift or arriving with him to work through the day. It was important to maintain a cheerful demeanor in public areas, particularly on days such as this one particular Tuesday when he looked quite haggard. The bright glow of his Idea had filled his whole night, leaving him sleepless and exhausted. The Idea! It was so evil that it nagged and pinched at him, so good he could not help but turn it over and over and over in his mind, admiring its facets.

Lieutenant Sanchez took pride in his creased, immaculate bearing at Lagrimas. He had purchased extra uniforms so that each day he could appear at work in fresh clothing. A prisoner he favored with extra conjugal visits spit-shined his shoes so brightly that they paled the best shines his Okinawan house-boys had ever been able to muster. He religiously performed his one hundred morning sit-ups in order to keep his encroaching belly at bay. He was sharp. There was no doubt in Lieutenant Sanchez' mind that being sharp had positioned him to be the Latino most rapidly promoted in the entire history of the Department of Corrections. Twenty years in the army and he had never made it beyond E-7, but after only three years here he had made Lieutenant!

He had made ruthless, even painful decisions in order to take advantage of opportunities. The most agonizing was his decision, reached after months of careful deliberation, to cut off his moustache. He had liked his moustache. It solidified his face, and added an element of taciturn menace to his heavily starched clothing. The problem was, every Mexican liked his moustache. He finally concluded that if he truly wanted to sound an executive note, the moustache would have to go.

The moustache went, and swept away with it all barriers to rapid advancement. Unfortunately, his rise had infuriated White officers who had waited long years for a lieutenant's slot to open, only to see him leap past them to fill it. Never mind that upper level staff was 99% White in a prison where Whites were a minority! The Whites had even gone to court, and sued him personally, along with the Director. He had approached the leader of the Association of Correctional Professionals and said, "Hey, look, I'm sorry you guys didn't get promoted too. What do you want me to do, turn it down?"

"If I were you," said Tarkenton, "I'd damn sure grab the promotion. Our beef is with the Director."

Sanchez was a member and Vice President of the newly formed Latino Correctional Officers Association. He could have been President, but did not want to be too strongly identified with a group that by its definition would always be a minority. On the other hand, he could not not be a member, and did not want to be present in any group merely as a spear-carrier. After due deliberation, he had elected to take the office of Vice President, and was pleased with his choice.

Sanchez viewed himself as a bridge between the White old-timers and the newly hired Mexican-Americans, but found it a tough and thankless task. The old guard complained that the minority hiring program was moving too fast; they told him, "We have no problem with minority hiring, if they get good people." He knew better. He had overheard their barbs, like, "They just lift up a taco and hire the first thing they see," before the laughter swallowed as he approached.

The new Chicano hires were very, very young, except for a few retired military like himself, and had chips on their shoulders a mile wide. He heard the sneers come out from behind their moustaches even when they were on their best behavior. Sometimes it was very hard for Lieutenant Sanchez to look at the bright side and stay in a good mood.

Sanchez' heroes were the Warden and the Director. The Warden was the stalwart knight of all the old guard. He was a big man who had come up through the ranks, had served his time. The Director had also come up through the ranks, but was often bitterly reviled by the old-timers, called a puppet under the sway of a cabal of deputy administrators who had never put in their time "in the pit, walking the yard". No doubt about it, minority hiring and promotions were the main reason the Director was sniped at.

The Warden had been very good to him, had taken him aside and complimented him on his promotion—the first administrator to compliment him—and had told him that he would be a cornerstone in the building of a new and better department. His eyes had glistened when he shook the Warden's hand and told the Warden that he, Lieutenant Sanchez, was one man the Warden could always count on.

He was thinking of the Warden when he finally reached the visiting wing and walked through the anteroom and down the small side corridor between offices to his office at the end. The Warden's picture on the wall behind his desk faced him when he opened the door. He took a lot of abuse for putting up that picture, but figured in the long run it would be worth it, and besides, what kind of man folded up because of a little teasing?

As he looked at the Warden's face, he remembered the poor man sprawled across the floor for all to see, with that college boy throwing papers at him. It was a ghastly, jarring sight.

Sanchez sat behind his desk, and riffled absently through the Bulletins and Directives in his In-basket while the Idea coursed through his mind. It had come to him suddenly and full-blown while driving home to Grapevine one afternoon through an unseasonable mist that reduced the sun to a watery, moon-like wafer. He could avenge the Warden, put an end to the inmates' union madness that was the only thing on anyone's mind lately, show the old guard that men like himself could take the initiative and *lead*, and justify his promotion in the minds of the doubters, all in one clear stroke. The only problem with his Idea was that it involved murder.

Sanchez finally decided to put the decision in the hands of fate. It was time to reach out. He needed the support of a key person, someone powerfully situated who had more to offer than an extra conjugal visit. Sanchez dialed the telephone number of Captain Crescimani, the Movement Chief. Crescimani might not back his play, but the captain was likely to listen sympathetically and admire him as a crazy Mexican with balls enough even if there was no deal.

✦

Big Man was not pleased by his summons to Sanchez' office. It could only be about his scheduled visit with Chino, or his trailer visit with his wife, and probably meant business problems. Business was always difficult. Being illegal meant that a steady 10-20% of product was captured, and several nonproductive people had to be paid. However, there were advantages. He did not have to spend millions of dollars a year in order to jack up demand like the purveyors of doped-up sugar water. The demand side was no problem at all. Big Man often likened himself to those Spanish entrepreneurs who financed voyages to the New World; many ships did not make it across the Atlantic and back, but if one did appear at the home docks laden with gold and chocolate and parrot feathers, there was enough money to buy a whole county.

Big Man moved carefully across the yard and into the main corridor. He and thirty-two other members of La Vida Loca had been abruptly moved from Folsom and San Quentin to Lagrimas the previous Christmas after two members had been stabbed by White Boys in San Quentin. He had been forced to order a hit on two White Boys in return, and had been rolled up from Folsom and sent to Lagrimas, a White Boys and los Berries stronghold. Nothing had happened yet; but the only reason for moving him to Lagrimas was to get him hurt.

Lagrimas housed hundreds of enemies. The only way he could see to avoid getting hurt was for an entire wing to be set aside for him and the others from Mexico and the Southwest, away from the White Boys and from the barrio gangs of Los Angeles and the Central Valley—especially los Berries. La Vida could also do business from a private wing by communicating with their families and paying off certain staff members. He had asked for a private wing, and twice been refused in spite of a very reasonable offer to the Captain in charge of placement. The old fuckers who run the penitentiary are supporting a monopoly, he thought, backing the play of gangs they had known for ages.

Los Berries from Los Angeles and organizations from the big valley in the middle of California were forty, fifty years old. Prisons had been an extension of their clubhouses for decades; when business started booming in the '50's, they were ready with connections for supply in Mexico and networks of distribution in place.

When he and his friends from Mexico, Texas, and the rest of the Southwest began taking care of each other, providing good product at fair prices, los Berries got ugly. Big Man appreciated the need for swift and certain retaliation when debts weren't paid—certainly no court would order a sheriff to collect—but the Berries' effort to freeze everyone out of their territory was unnecessary greed. His people had gotten hurt; some were killed.

He had gone to the young Blacks who were just getting started and offered to supply them quality product at a very good price, and when they were skeptical, he and Chino had taken out Pancho, the Berries' leader in Folsom, and left two others on the floor. The Blacks closed the deal. Big Man skated free, but they buried Chino in the Hole at Folsom for years and years. Big Man crossed himself and thanked God Chino was finally on the streets, coordinating imports and distribution to the towns and prisons and work camps and jails supplied by La Vida. No one was more capable.

Los Berries had aligned themselves with the White Boys, and the war was on, had been on now for nine years, mostly a cold war with occasional fights and price wars, never so bad as to shut things down for any length of time. They had finally carved out the right to do business.

Lagrimas would be a good place to work from. It was centrally located in the valley, and would mesh well with their strength in the San Francisco Bay area and around Los Angeles, but they would be wiped out if they started to deal here from the main line. They needed the wing. La Vida lived in danger all the time. The Union was dominating the pen lately; everybody wondered if it would be a good thing, how it might affect business. Magon told him it would have nothing to do with business, would not hurt or help. Nobody was getting hurt in the meantime, but that would pass, times of peace always came to an end.

Big Man pushed open the door to the visiting wing, and walked past old Robinson and two "model prisoners," one a Vida member. He turned down the short hall of glassed-in offices and stood at Sanchez' door. Sanchez waved him right in.

Five minutes later he left the office to find his top lieutenants. Sanchez had given him something unexpected: a surprise.

Big Man stood with his men waiting for a game on the basketball court. Lowering skies charged the air with an urgency that infected the ball games and exercises.

"So Sanchez says we can have a wing, eh, for killing someone hooked up out front with the Union."

"Right."

"What's his trip, man?"

"I think he's frontin' for the Warden."

"On the level?"

"It's a big step for him to talk to me."

"That's one of four people, right?"

"One of three. We can't fuck with Fred Johnson 'cause he's identified with the Brotherhood enough to muddy the waters about why he got hit."

"He'd be a tough motherfucker to take out, too."

"The Fly is working on our transfer lawsuit, right?"

"Right."

"I'd like to get that White dude, the big college kid, you know?"

Big Man shook his head. He knew all along who it would have to be. "He's had his face in the papers before he came here. There'd be stories in the news, on TV, a whole lotta sniffing around if he gets hurt. The stories could go different directions, some of them very bad. Do you want to become Public Enemy # 1? Could we stand the heat? You guys have gotta look down as well as up when you're making plans, think about what we could lose as well as what we could gain."

A pause stretched out until it was filled with what had to come.

"How about Magon?"

Handballs ricocheted through the silence that followed the mention of Magon's name. The objections raised against the other three did not apply. Magon was closely identified with the Union, and with no one else. He had no essential skills, no powerful connections. He was a friend, but being from the Central Valley, he wasn't family. After a long moment, Big Man said, "I want to feel out what would come down from the people who started the Union off if we take out Magon. Be here tomorrow, same time."

Fred Johnson was easy to find these days; he ran several laps at the same time each morning, and hung out on the yard to talk until lunchtime. Big Man smoked a Camel while he watched Fred complete his finishing kick and caught up with him as he walked, arms held high, dripping sweat.

"Freddie, how you doin'."

"Big Man! Good to see you, man. Walk with me while I catch my breath."

The two walked around the grass in the middle of the track. Two White Boys came puffing toward them, gasping for air. Fred patted Big Man on the back as they went by. "You know, it's always good talkin' with you, and I like to be seen with you every now and then, too. Since I been workin' for the Union, some people tryin' to hang a White Boy jacket on me. How you like this pen?"

"Well, it ain't the friendliest place I ever been."

"We're tryin to keep the lid on 'round here. I know you got to feel like a fish floppin' on dry land."

Big Man probed Johnson's loyalties as gently as he could, like pulling a thistle from a Doberman's paw, with questions about when the Brotherhood's next Open House would be and what the Union was up to.

"The Union is goin' to court to try to get formally recognized inside this pen. They're gonna call me and Carruthers and Magon out to testify! Ain't that a bitch!? The Fly don't think we got much of a chance, but I tell you, man, that woman Teresa can talk a cat out of its claws when she gets goin'."

Johnson suddenly stopped walking and looked at Big Man with a level, almost pushy gaze. "The Brotherhood is my people, and the Union means the world to me. A few other brothers, not many, but a few of the *best*, feel the same way. I love 'em both, and the people who are out front are as precious to me as my own mother. If anything was to happen to your mother, you wouldn't stop to count the cost, would you, you would just start comin'."

Johnson had felt his probes pinch. Big Man spoke promptly. "Hey, the Union had made some great moves, man." He slapped Johnson softly on the shoulder and smiled. "I'm a paid-up member, man, like most everybody in La Vida. I can't afford to have nothin' get started here—a handful of my people are stuck here way out on a limb, we're so outnumbered that we could each take ten people with us and still get buried. We *need* somethin' like the Union, even more than you do. I'm glad to hear that you'll be staying with it."

He had mollified Johnson, but the conversation made him lose his taste for the proposition. It would not work. Damage to Magon would bring the Brotherhood down on them, and license los Berries and White Boys to do what they already were inclined to do, along with anybody else who supported the Union. There were now thousands of Union members, God knows who might come at them out of the woodpile. They could easily be creamed before any Wing ever materialized. Fly would also fuck up their lawsuit. It was ill-advised, a great deal of risk for an uncertain reward.

Big Man met with his lieutenants the following morning on schedule, and told them it was out of the question. It was an unpopular reversion. They groused and grumbled—they were tired of always looking over their shoulder—but eventually came around. The hierarchical structure of La Vida Loca left no room for dissent.

Sanchez was a more delicate matter. He had obviously crossed a lot of bridges in order to make the offer, and might well be upset at having done so for no reason. Big Man appeared in Sanchez' office the following day. He couched his refusal in a setting of great appreciation for Sanchez's offer. Before he finished, Sanchez held up both hands, palms facing Big Man, and said, "No, no, no need to explain. I understand. It was only an offer that I felt would be in our mutual best interests, but who knows? Perhaps not. I only ask that—"

"Don't worry for a second. No one will talk."

"Thank you. Now, I have other business to attend to before noon. . . ."

Big Man left the office troubled. Sanchez had surprised him a second time by his indifference to the outcome of his offer. It was all very strange.

Big Man never liked surprises, especially from people like Sanchez who had always been predictable.

Angel Gutierrez could barely control his anger at Big Man's decision to pass on Sanchez' offer. As soon as it was permissible to leave the meeting he broke away from the handball court and hit the track running, oblivious to who was around him. The sky was shaded by gray and white clouds lumbering north, an unseasonably late storm, and the track glistened from last night's rain.

The muggy air and fast pace sent sweat streaming down Angel's body. Big Man was a fool. He had grown cowardly in his old age, he no longer had vision. Big Man wasn't in any real danger, his reputation shielded him, but he, Angel, known to be a lieutenant for many years, smaller and prettier than he ought to be, was a very prime target. Goddamn it, they needed the wing. It would keep them safe. They could begin to do business, supply product to their natural market from a protected position. Fuck the Berries! They had no right to a monopoly here. . . . Angel's heaving lungs intruded on his thoughts and shouted at him he had completed the first lap too fast. He slowed down.

La Vida was in real danger of being wiped out here, and of missing a tremendous opportunity. He had heard that some White Boys had gotten hurt in Mazatlan trying to retrieve a large yacht for a San Francisco bank from a purchaser who had not kept up the payments. Just the kind of services La Vida could provide far better than Gringo slobs who didn't know where the hell they were. . . .

Big Man, the immovable stone, the solid rock in their path, was satisfied with the same slow, steady growth, a new branch every year, Bakersfield this year, Modesto the next, Sacramento after that; but the time was ripe for a leap up and out of their ruts and a shift of gears into another level—the provision of a broad range of goods and services to individuals, corporations, and governments all over the hemisphere!

Angel kept himself pure. He had never even touched a White person, and could not fathom mixing himself with a filthy, smelly, noisy, screeching Black one like Magon did—and not even hiding his perversion! Magon *deserved* to die. Killing him would be easy. Magon was educated, superficially different from most brown people, but scratch him lightly and he was the same fatalistic small-timer at heart. If they timed it to happen within a day or two of a move to a private Wing. . . . Johnson was a threat, he had no reason to dispute Big Man's account of their meeting, but Angel suspected that not many other members of the Brotherhood felt the same way. He could hire others to kill Magon, people unconnected with La Vida Loca. It was risky, but no risk, no reward . . . he veered left to pass lollygagging White Boys, and envisioned them parting like the sea to make way for his final victorious kick across the tape. He was getting no younger. Big Man never would age or change at all. He would go see Sanchez himself.

Sweat streamed from Angel's body as he left the track and walked around the handball court. He sat against the court, his narrow back to the wall, and looked out through a wide green stucco tunnel formed by the walls of the wings on either side and over the yard that lay before him: grass, dirt track, asphalt for basketball, and a clear shot ahead to faraway eucalyptus trees and a darkening sky. The double cyclone fences and coiled barbed wire in the distance were invisible from here, his favorite spot.

Angel lifted his eyes to follow a red-tailed hawk that drifted sideways across the yard. The hawk abruptly surged up and straight out with two mighty movements of his wings that sounded in Angel's ears like a chorus. No one else seemed to notice the predator's flight. He would be great, or he would fail and die, but he would not, could not drift unnoticed through life and then die without a murmur.

Angel went to the visiting wing but could not get through the door without a ducat. He asked to see Lieutenant Sanchez and told the gate guard that it was important. The gate guard yawned. Angel waited in the hall, hoping to catch Sanchez on his way home at 3:30.

At 3:30 there was no sign of Sanchez. It was perilously close to Count, when he had to be present in his cell. He waited until nine minutes before Count, one minute over his minimum time necessary to make it back to his cell, and was turning to leave as Sanchez came out the door.

Angel approached the Lieutenant and spoke quickly, in Spanish.

"I need to speak with you about your offer to Big Man yesterday."

"Bullshit. I don't know what you—"

"Big Man is going to refuse when he sees you tomorrow." Sanchez flushed briefly, and continued walking.

"I can get the job done for you, on the same terms."

After four more quick steps, Sanchez turned and looked at Angel for the first time.

"I can explain in the morning before school and after count in your office."

Sanchez' pace quickened again. Angel matched his strides. They passed Fred Johnson dressed in his barber's smock hurrying to his afternoon's work in the staff barber shop.

"What's the matter, Lieutenant, don't you like it around here?" Fred's eyes were twinkling, noticing.

Sanchez broke into a strained smile. "Eight hours a day is enough for me. See you in the shop."

"I'm always ready," Johnson hollered over his shoulder as he walked past.

The day shift was moving out, the swing shift was at its post, convicts were in their rooms. Angel did not know what to do.

"Eight o'clock tomorrow, my office." He didn't turn his head or break his stride when he spoke. Angel nodded, and broke into a sprint. He made it home with no time to spare.

"Man, you playin it on the edge," said the young, lithe Black guard just assigned to his wing.

"Just so I don't fall off, right?" Angel opened his cell door, nodded to his cellie, and stood to be counted.

16

THE HOSTILE EXCHANGE BETWEEN ART AND TERESA ECHOED IN Robert's mind for several days after, and soured his work. He perfunctorily answered the mail, taking as his own the tedium of saying No over and over and over to endless requests for legal help.

Art had once viewed such mail as an opportunity. "Tell 'em they've got to organize!" he boomed as he showed Robert how to answer the mail. "Put it right back on 'em. The Union helps those who help themselves." Art wasn't booming these days. He was rarely around the office. Twice Robert approached him to talk, but veered away at the last minute. Robert decided to avoid Teresa and her harshness. It was easier to do than he would have liked; she was preoccupied with preparing for the hearing in Grapevine on the lawsuit.

In fact, Robert noticed that he was lonely. At one time everyone in the Union had enjoyed an occasional evening out or day trip around the Bay Area with him; he was grateful to be taken anywhere, he listened carefully, looked closely wherever one pointed, and expressed no annoying opinions on where to go or how long to stay. However, his novelty value had apparently waned. For the first time since coming west two and a half years earlier Robert thought of returning to Louisville, but disenchantment with his life in California did little to refurbish his image of home.

He must lack that crucial something that makes people take you seriously. What the hell was it? After a long breather, he was again preoccupied with his own shortcomings, chiefly with his youth. He had not yet done anything worth noticing, or lived enough to know anything. He had no ethnic or religious identity to define him or supply a historical mission. He really did not yet exist.

"Robert, what's the matter?"

Jarred from his reverie, he looked up at Teresa standing on the other side of his desk.

"Let's go get some coffee," she said.

They walked half a block to the ice cream store on the corner.

"Are you mad at me?" she asked.

"I don't know, you got pretty fuckin' brutal the other night."

"Do you think what Art said to me was nice? He was pretty fuckin' brutal, too. Everybody treats Art like he's a force of nature, but they expect me to be always compassionate and understanding. Well, I can't pull it off."

Robert sipped an unfamiliar espresso as she talked, and felt it burn through him.

"Art's a good man," she said, "but he's liable to fall off the ladder just like the rest of us. I guess I thought that if I hit him over the head with a 2×4, he might snap out of his—his resentment and tiredness, but that was a rationalization, a reason to say what I wanted to say. I'm sorry it happened. I talked to Art and Myrna last night. Its OK between us—not great, but OK, good enough to get us through the hearing."

Teresa had been looking around; now, she settled her gaze on him. "This hearing will have at least ten witnesses, and a dozen motions to research, write and type. Just the mechanical job of getting our four prisoner witnesses delivered to court requires the preparation of orders, getting them signed by a judge and delivered to the sheriff and the warden, all of whom are 150 miles away. I've never done anything like this. It's not beyond me to figure out, but I'm not efficient. It could swallow all our money and keep half our office engaged full-time, but if I hit on you and Myrna—or Art—at some point I become the lawyer sponge soaking up all our resources, and bring all Art's lawyer nightmares into reality. If I don't, then I have to work long hours every day for weeks."

"Maybe it's just too big for us."

"Maybe. You don't know until you try."

Robert was startled to see that she had lost weight, a lot of weight. Her skin was dull, her eyes encased in shadows—and he had not noticed though he saw her every day. Where had he been? He reached across the table and touched her wrist. "Let's go for a walk," he said.

They climbed slowly up the hill behind their building. When they reached the small park on top he turned around and looked back north over the roofs of the houses they had passed to the towers of downtown San Francisco, distant and silent like a movie set, and the looping concrete that brought fresh blood to the city center and took away enervated bodies at the close of the day. A worm of fog undulated inland beneath the Golden Gate Bridge, and a huge fog bank strained against Twin Peaks to the west; tufts of fog broke off and sailed straight toward them over the valley of the Mission District.

Wind roared above them through cypress trees. Robert inhaled sharply, and said, "This city is so lucky to have ocean breezes that shove all the shit in the air east, so beautiful. . . . Do you think people who have always lived here know how great it is?"

"Nah." Teresa grinned. "They're plenty arrogant about living here, but only because of what they read in the paper. It takes provincials like us to really savor the place."

Robert shivered, and took Teresa's hand. He touched the smile lines and other wrinkles in the corners of her eyes, and looked through her eyes and saw that part of her that had not altered a jot since she was seven years old, and would never change at all.

He did not lower his eyes as was his custom when she looked at him. A lovely young man, she thought, very sweet, delicious. Many times before she had been faithful to her desire to make love, and later been appalled as everything went horribly wrong, almost in exact proportion to the pleasure and warmth experienced, like a perverse law of nature. It always seemed a treacherous surrender to convention not to act on such feelings, and later a heedless ignorance to have carried them through. Over and over she had been stunned by this reversal. She did not understand it, but was lately beaten by a series of confusions and resentments into a reluctant acceptance that it was the way of the world. But Robert was almost thirteen years younger than she, so much younger that the danger of couple expectations was really unthinkable. . . .

She parted her lips just slightly, and Robert's soul came out from hiding and moved to the surface of his skin. His hand touched her cheek as he leaned forward to kiss her, and his fingers pressed on to bury themselves in her hair.

They turned without speaking and walked slowly together down the hill. Teresa's body tingled where brushed by her clothes, and her nipples pressed hard against the cloth that covered them.

She felt her muscles flex, and gritted her teeth to keep from bursting into flames before they reached her room above the office.

17

The Fly's Journal
—July 4, 1976

It was my day off. Magon was coming to see me. I didn't bother wondering for long why those two convicts were hanging around in the hall; convicts often have the air of people going nowhere. It was a nice morning, the air still cool down on the first floor. I was playing with my mail and my files, making lists, reviewing my testimony for next week's hearing. Fred Johnson's petition had been denied by the district court, and I had asked him to come by while Magon and I played our Friday morning chess game.

I was searching for my clear plastic letter opener—an instrument that I had written innumerable in-house appeals in support of and regained twice after it was confiscated—when I heard scuffling in the hall. The instant I found my letter-opener I heard a cry for help, loud, hopeless, the sound of a man going down for the third and last time. The cry drove the two guards sitting in their office at the end of the hall across from my cell closer to their back wall, as far from the office door as they could get, and deeper into the sheets of paper in front of them.

I was off my bunk and on the bars. From the extreme right side of my cell I could see halfway up the corridor, far enough to see that Magon was being stuck. The drifting convicts I had seen earlier were on each of his arms, and one behind who I could not see landed cutting blows that sounded like deep stabs.

I hollered to the guards, who I could see clear as a bell through the glass in their bright snotgreen room, but they buried their noses deeper in paper and ignored me. Ignorant Ignorantines, fat fearful smokers of infinite numbers of cigarettes, drinkers of bottomless vats of coffee, they sit all day sweating and scleroticizing, terror and hate skirmishing in their eyes, blood pressure rising while they wait with their breath held for twenty years to pass and ripen into a pension behind their semi-permeable glass wall that allows them to hear only what they want to hear—Scum dressed in tinsel, drying in the sun.

Magon began to fall. The man who was stabbing him came into view, and suddenly turned. Fred Johnson came running toward him. As Fred approached, the knifer lunged at him. Fred turned sideways as he flew by; the knifer missed. Fred leapt over one convict and seemed to have run past everybody, but his left arm snaked out behind him for the face of the knifer and whipped forward toward me, pulling the knifer over backwards, over Magon's slumping body so hard that the back of the knifer's head, the first part of his body to hit the floor, exploded with a sickening crunch that echoed off the walls and drove one guard even closer to his own wall—the other, horrified, froze solid.

A blade embedded in clear resinous plastic came clattering down the hall and settled a few feet from my cell. I tried to reach it with a legal-sized envelope, but the Mexican I had seen loitering moments before came running and stumbling down on the floor and snatched it. He turned back and faced the thumps and gurgling, strangled cries coming from the other end of the hall. The Mexican quickly regained his breath and impassive expression. He didn't move backward or forward but stood still, both arms lifted, one holding the knife, eyes down the hall. The door to the main corridor opened and closed two or three times, but no one entered. Our floor stayed very quiet.

Fred came close and the two began to stalk. Fred made feints toward the Mexican and the Mexican reached out with his blade but never committed himself. He was a very good knife fighter, experienced and calm. The two continued to circle each other, and I saw one guard finally reach for the phone and make a call.

Fred's adrenalin was fading and the Mexican's confidence was gathering; after all, he did have the knife. Unfortunately for him, he also carried the weight of *machismo* and when I told him in Spanish, the first words uttered since Magon's cry for help, that he loved to suck the cock of the man who fucked his mother, he glanced toward me.

Fred's timing was perfect. He surged forward and grabbed the

Mexican's forearm with his two huge hands, one on the wrist and the other just beneath the elbow, and drove the forearm down with both hands onto his rising knee. The knife bounced off the concrete floor again, and Fred brought the heel of his palm up and into the Mexican's nose. Blood gushed from his face as the Mexican slumped to the floor.

Fred stood still for a moment, his eyes unfocussed, and then moved back up the hall. He was kneeling by Magon when staff began to pour through the far door. Their cries were the signal for our craven lardbutts to charge out of their office so fast that one slipped on the Mexican's blood and fell, and when he realized why he had fallen he became nauseated and added to the fluids coating the concrete floor. And some say our species is the culmination, the leading edge of the evolutionary process. I say, Let's roll the dice again.

"A single spark can start a prairie fire," said Mao Tse Tung. True enough, if the day is hot and it hasn't rained in months. He coined that image illustrating the power of one person or a small group to transform the face of society in order to firm the resolve of his badly outnumbered comrades. To me, however, it illustrates that the oldest grandest forest on the continent or the most inspiring man-made structure can be destroyed by one asshole with a little gasoline and a match. Jack London sank the better part of his fortune and most of his heart into a glorious house, and never recovered his spirit after staring at its ashes the morning after the building was completed.

Our goal of due process of law is too flimsy to bear the awful weight of death. Our means—fellowship and imagination, daring enterprise within tight constraints—are smeared over with blood, lost. We will not recover.

It is past midnight. I talked to three guards today, and told them nothing. However, I asked Huff to come back and see me after I meet with Teresa. I'm going to violate the sacred Convict Code and tell everything I saw. Otherwise it's curtains for Fred. It may not help, but I'm basically in no mood to be quiet.

There is an eerie peace now, a restoration of equilibrium. Violence frightens most people here, but as an institution this prison needs violence; not too much, not too little. It squeaks and cracks without its ration. The whole order of things here is set up with violence in mind. Without it, things begin to look silly. Hushed voices are murmuring all around the prison, telling how it had to happen. The experts, and there is no guard or convict who is not an expert, nod knowingly to each other and say they saw it coming. There is a palpable calm now; not so much the quiet of the graveyard as the numbness of the familiar. Blood is the oil of the prison machinery. It's been long overdue for a lube job.

18

ANGEL MOVED AGAINST THE FLOW TOWARD THE VISITING WING, AND wondered why Sanchez had summoned him. When he reached the door, the guard at the gate told him that the whole institution was being locked down because of some trouble, and all visits were suspended. He showed the guard his ducat authorizing a visit with Lt. Sanchez.

"Magon is still alive", said Sanchez. His tone was distracted, his body rigid behind his desk.

"That's not right, I saw him get stuck deep a bunch of times."

"It *is* right. He's at Community Hospital."

It had never occurred to Angel that Magon might survive the attack. He had been indifferent when Magon walked by on the yard last week as he negotiated the hit and paid off Skoog, a man known to Magon and everyone else as a professional killer. Angel's gut wrenched at the thought of Magon identifying him in court, and twisted tighter at an image of Magon's mocking face. "Let me make a phone call," he said to Sanchez.

"No. You've lost some people, but you've done your job, more than your job. Fred Johnson is going away for a murder beef. Your wing is coming. Now—"

"Magon saw me."

Sanchez paused. "You can't use the phone. The whole pen is locked down."

"Let's stop playing games, Lieutenant. You're in this up to your eyes. Let me make a phone call, and neither of us needs to worry."

The phone rang several times before Chino answered. Sanchez rose from behind his desk as Angel began to explain what needed to be done, and walked out of his office.

Chino questioned him closely, but finally accepted Angel's asserted authority as Big Man's agent. Magon would be finished off within 24 hours.

As Angel hung up the phone the office door swung open. He turned, and hid surprise as best he could when he saw it was not Sanchez but the young Black guard from his wing.

"What's going on?" the guard demanded.

Angel stretched a silence as long as he could before it snapped, and had inhaled to speak when Sanchez hurried back and drew the guard's attention.

"Did you know this guy was here?"

"Oh yeah, I let him call his family to tell them all visits are cancelled. What's up?"

The guard relaxed, and so did Angel.

"Word from the warden is that Teresa Suchil has scheduled attorney visits with a lot of people, but no attorney visits are permitted. Another lawyer's up all the way from LA, he can't get in either. Its a real tight lockdown. Man, there was ambulances lined up out front like convicts in a chow line."

Sanchez waved Angel on and said, "Back to your Wing, Gutierrez," and turned his whole attention to the young guard. "Yeah, you know, the December '73 lockdown lasted for four months—things *still* aren't back to normal . . ." Sanchez was cool, no visible trace of guilt or stress other than the film of sweat glistening on his upper lip.

19

She walked through a high meadow, part of a wiggling unbroken line of people that reached over the highest of several crests ahead. The sky was purest blue, the outline of tall conifers and mountains sharply etched. She stepped off the trail and rested for a moment on the grass. It was the middle of the day. What will they eat for lunch, she thought, seeing that the strolling people, pleased at being on level ground, carried no packs on their backs, and had empty hands. Where will they sleep? She looked about, and realized that she was clad only in sandals, a skirt, and short-sleeved blouse, and carried nothing with her.

The alarm clock jarred Teresa awake and out of her dream. She groped through the dark, turned it off, and lay still for a moment, eyes closed, drawing out a sweet limbo as long as possible before an invading sight, sound, or thought triggered a memory of who she was supposed to be. The faint smell of orange peels by her mattress reminded her of her morning's appointments in Lagrimas.

Although her room was cold and she had far to go, she lingered a moment to look out her north window. Enveloped by darkness and mist, the distant corporate headquarters, advertising signs, and vehicles lost all definition; what remained were random rows and columns of shimmering white and orange lights, moving white and red lights that appeared and disappeared, and a diadem of light along the foreshortened arch of the Bay Bridge topped by a red beacon that pulsed regularly every few seconds. The view, an extraordinary, unexpected pleasure, her chief luxury and distraction, had absorbed many hours and arrested her every day. She would miss it.

All the necessaries for her trip were laid out on the windowseat, faithfully waiting: pants, underwear, sandals, blouse, tweed jacket, and a wide-brimmed straw hat; yellow legal pad, three pens, a file folder that held the petition, witness questions, blank paper, numbered court paper, four letters from her clients, and a letter from Lagrimas confirming her visit. Her journal and a slim volume of poetry were for the dead time, driver's license and proof of admission to the California State Bar were ready for presentation, and she had a handful of dimes should there be any difficulties. It would be her last visit to prepare her prisoner witnesses for the hearing due to begin on Monday, three days hence.

Teresa quickly bathed and dressed, filled her thermos with coffee, and slid quietly through glass doors that opened to the back deck. Her car was parked in front of the building. Art had cleaned and repainted the scruffy aquamarine machine a bright midnight blue shortly after her arrival in San Francisco. The smooth dark gleam of her most constant companion of the previous several years was still a shock.

Art had been so happy to have her. . . . Teresa grimaced, and started her car.

She was soon over the Bay Bridge and on the freeway east bound for the Central Valley, three hours south. Teresa did not mind at all this term of confinement. Driving on the freeways could be relegated to automatic pilot, and she savored the chance to let her thoughts wander. The sight of the prison, like imminent death, could be trusted to concentrate her mind wonderfully.

A dull glow silhouetted the ridgeline to the east. As she drove over the ridgetop, the valley below was bathed in purple, a lovely dawn artifact of the summer smog. The air later turned a dingy gray-brown when the sun rose high and hot.

Nights with Robert had become a sweet habit. The poor boy still thought she was doing him a favor by sleeping with him. Teresa did not know how long she could maintain a facade of easy indifference, or what would happen when it fell.

She left the freeway south of Modesto and drove along a full irrigation ditch. The ditches all around her Central Valley childhood were the site of mysterious drownings, sudden deaths of field workers chased by men in uniforms, and zones of forbidden pleasure, where she and her brother swam on hot afternoons close to shady banks in spite of her mother's dire warnings. She looked forward to buying fresh peaches, apricots, figs, almonds, and golden raisins on her way back, and she would relish even more leaving the Valley behind in the afternoon, sloughing it off again in favor of San Francisco.

The one-mile approach to the prison through fields of vegetables and fruit trees was bordered on both sides by tall, closely planted eucalyptus trees that created a dark tunnel illuminated by soft tubes of light filled with glittering dust. Teresa left her jacket in the car and walked across the parking lot. The small shed-roofed entrance building broke the course of two high cyclone fences topped with coiled barbed wire that ran twenty feet apart around the main building. It was the only legitimate way in or out.

Women and children waited inside. There was no movement. She pushed through to the front desk.

"Hi, Teresa!" The visiting officer was a young woman who had come to work at the prison at about the same time Teresa first came to visit.

"Hi, Margaret. What's going on?"

"I don't know. They called and told me not to let anybody through till further notice. That was an hour ago. I guess since you're a lawyer and have those appointments, you can go on back, but I don't know if you'll see anybody."

"You haven't heard anything at all?"

"Not a peep. Wasn't nothin' wrong when I came on this morning, either."

"If you find out anything, let me know, alright?"

"All right."

Teresa showed her papers and took off her shoes. She walked through the metal detector without tripping its squeal, picked up her goods, and waited until Margaret pushed the button that opened the back door. She stepped outside and waited in front of a 20-foot high gate through the inner cyclone fence until a gun tower guard noticed her and chose to hit the only switch capable of opening the gate.

She walked along a sidewalk past nine wings of the prison and turned into V-Wing. The visiting room was empty; no steamy clinches, no squalling children. The only other person there was a close-cropped sergeant she had not seen before. After standing by the man's desk to insure that he called the right wing with the right message she sat down and waited.

The inevitable, interminable waiting had driven her to the edge of sanity when she began visiting prisoners. She had searched for solace by thinking of the far greater ordeals endured by women in other parts of waited for information on such fundamental questions as whether their family members were alive or dead, but found none. The feeling of suffocating helplessness, the fog of bureaucratic malice and indifference, remained.

After thirty minutes she rose from her seat and walked to the desk. "Please call C and F wing and ask them what the problem is."

"I already called."

"Please call again. All four of my clients knew I was coming this morning"—she showed him four letters—"and know how to make themselves available."

The sergeant heaved an elaborate sigh, and picked up the phone. "Walters in Visiting. What about Johnson and the others?" A pause. "Oh, yeah? Who was it? None of 'em? Okay." He hung up the phone and turned to Teresa. "None of 'em can come out today."

"Why not?"

"*I* don't know. That's what the man said. They don't tell me anything around here."

Teresa looked at him steadily as he spoke. She then turned and walked outdoors into a bright blast of heat and fertilizer stench. Whistles from unseen prisoners bounced off unnoticed. Warnings and premonitions leapt out of their box in the back of her mind and whined around her like angry mosquitoes. No one was in the Entrance Building other than the visiting officer.

"Teresa, they tell you anything?"

"Not yet. See you in a minute."

Teresa went out to the pay phone attached to the side of the building. She took three deep breaths, exhaled as much air as she could, and dialed the Warden's office.

"I'd like to speak with the Warden, please."

"May I tell him who's calling?"

"Teresa Suchil, attorney for Sergio Magon, Nathan Steiner, Fred Johnson, and David Carruthers."

"Thank you." In two minutes the secretary returned.

"The Warden is tied up now. May I have your number and ask him to return your call?"

Teresa launched herself like a skier down a precipice. "Tell the Warden that if I don't call my San Francisco office within thirty minutes, it will call every newspaper, television and news radio station in Northern California, as well as every legislative office, the Director of Corrections in Sacramento, and any other media representative and superior state official they can think of, to say that four prisoners due to testify against the Warden in court next week have been hidden by him and have been cut off from their attorney. While they are calling I will be on my way to the courthouse to seek an order that they be immediately produced. Do you follow me?"

"Well. . ."

"I'm waiting at the pay phone by the side of the Entrance Building and will be here until eleven o'clock."

"Very good, Ms. Suchil," said the secretary in her frozen-sweet popsicle voice. "I'll inform the warden of your feelings."

"Spare him my feelings. You can remind him that it is very hot out here in the world and I won't wait an extra minute." Teresa hung up the phone, and answered it five minutes later.

The short path to the Administration Wing was bordered by old, carefully tended rose bushes in full bloom. Their sweet smell sorely tempted Teresa to lower her nose into one of the yellow or deep red flowers, but she pressed on. The Warden's secretary met her at the door. The secretary was quite young, dressed in bright polyester and white patent leather sandals. "Ms. Suchil I presume?" the secretary smiled a shallow smile. Teresa nodded and extended her hand. The secretary reflexively reached toward it, hesitated, and continued on to shake it.

The two women walked past office pools of neon light and weary secretaries sitting like wilted lilies at desks between ancient metal filing cabinets partially covered with chipped paint and torn bulletins. They climbed stairs protected with No-Skid rubber matting worn through to the linoleum beneath, and turned back toward the front of the building. The walls of the second floor hall were covered with paintings by the resident prisoners: saguaro cacti at sunset, nude women with gravity-defying breasts on black velvet, bucolic oils of weathered barns and fenceposts on the edge of untended meadows.

They came to a barred gate across the hall. The secretary pressed a button; a portion of the gate hummed and popped open. The Warden's office loomed ahead, on the second floor just above the wing's entrance. He had no doubt watched her enter the building.

"Good morning, Ms. Suchil. Please come in."

The Warden was a very large, pale, jowly man, well over six feet tall. His body spilled out of his cuffs and collar and over his belt. He extended a huge thick-fingered hand covered with rings. She took it for an instant as she stood, and shuddered as she felt a charged cold dampness, as if she had touched an eel. He's nothing more or less than a man, she reminded herself, and walked with him into a dark, cool, immaculate office.

"Sit down, please. I understand you're concerned about your clients, and I'm sorry about the problems we've had today. There was a fight in the wing where they all live. Several people were hurt. One is dead. Another three are seriously injured."

Teresa sat paralyzed, suspended between wanting to know every detail and wanting to stay within the version of reality she had brought with her to Lagrimas.

"We don't know yet whether it was a race problem or gangs or what it was about. We've had to lock down the entire prison. I'm not supposed to say anything about who is hurt until an effort is made to notify the families, but I did some checking while waiting for you. One of the people hurt was Sergio Magon."

"How badly?" she cried quickly, in the instant before her throat locked tight.

The Warden cleared his throat, and ignored her question. "You understand, nobody's doing any visits now or for the next several days while we investigate. It's my job to keep this place safe for everybody who lives and works here. I know we have an obligation to make the inmates available for attorney visits, and I've directed our staff to let you in tomorrow morning." His voice was growing steadily louder.

"My office is in San Francisco. Today is Friday. Our hearing begins on Monday." Teresa drew a measure of strength from her recitation of facts. "I need to see them now, especially if anyone is suspected of being involved in criminal activity, or is in any way hurt."

"I'm sorry, I'm not going to endanger my staff or other inmates for your convenience, I just won't do it. I think I've bent over backwards in allowing you to visit tomorrow, and I can tell you this, young woman, I know of several occasions when we've locked this place down tight and haven't let any lawyers in for two weeks or more, and we can do it again."

A hand floated into her body and formed a fist around her heart. "Warden, all four of these men are material witnesses. I've got to try to obtain an order from the court that I be allowed to see them as soon as possible. As a conscientious person, I think you would do the same if you were me."

"Perhaps." The Warden stood up, and Teresa followed. "I'm sure the judge will find our position of allowing you in tomorrow morning a reasonable one, not deserving of a high-handed order that won't reach me until tomorrow anyway. Thank you." Beneath his formal correctness, the Warden's voice had reached a deafening volume.

Teresa was immensely relieved to escape the freezer locker morgue of an office and feel the warmth outside. The concrete sidewalk shimmered in the heat. Its reflected light stung her eyes.

As she walked toward her car, she spotted an ambulance waiting quietly by the vehicle entrance at the far end of the deserted parking lot.

"Lady, you're blockin' the driveway," the driver said as she approached the ambulance and parked behind it.

"I'll move in just a minute. I'm an attorney for one of the men that was hurt." Teresa reached in her wallet for ID as she spoke. "He's supposed to be in court Monday, and I need to see him to know what to tell the Judge."

"My job is to run 'em in. We don't have no time for no interviews."

"Where will they be taken?"

The driver's gaze travelled slowly up and down her body. For the ten thousandth time in her life, Teresa gritted her teeth and held her tongue.

"To the hospital," he finally said.

"Which hospital?" Teresa didn't bother to unclench her teeth.

"How about Community Hospital?" The ambulance driver grinned. A siren sounded in the distance, and guards appeared to open the gate.

"How about it? How about it?" Teresa's eyes darted quickly to the name on the side of the ambulance and back to the driver's face. "If it's not Community, you'll spend a couple of hours under oath in court telling me why you lied."

"Take it easy, lady," he said, lower lip protruding. "It's Community."

The gate swung open and the driver took his ambulance through. Another in the distance, its red light flashing and siren swelling, closed rapidly. Teresa jumped into her truck and headed toward Grapevine. As she drove, she envisioned the ambulance driver together with beer-drinking buddies burping and griping about goddamned bitches. Rage flooded her, along with a horribly violent image of herself blowing his head off with a shotgun. It left her drained when it receded, gripping her steering wheel and wondering how she would get through a day that had not yet reached noon.

The Warden's offer of entry into prison the next morning, as he had accurately pointed out, could be withdrawn in a second. At the public typing room of her old junior college she prepared an Order, with all the proper flourishes. Ten minutes later, she arrived downtown at the Grapevine County courthouse.

The chambers of Judge William Pedrocelli were on the fourth floor of the Annex, a huge beige stucco and dark glass rectangle that dwarfed the old Corinthian-columned original courthouse and transformed it from a symbol of classical rationality and cultural continuity into a warty protuberance. A criminal trial had recessed, and all parties, spectators, and jury members were out to lunch. Teresa waited in the anteroom of the judge's chambers until 1:20, when His Honor returned. She remained seated; he was very short, and sensitive about his height.

"Good afternoon, Ms. Suchil."

"Good afternoon, your Honor. It's good to see you."

The Judge's secretary entered the office, and smiled at Teresa.

"I have a conference on jury instructions to complete before closing arguments, which are due to start in ten minutes."

"I know you're busy. I wouldn't be here if it weren't important."

"What's the problem?"

"I can't get into Lagrimas to see any of my witnesses. The Warden told me one of them was involved in a violent incident. He said he might be hurt, but wouldn't tell me exactly. He said he wouldn't let me in until tomorrow morning."

"What's wrong with that?"

Teresa looked past the judge to his secretary, an elderly woman who had always treated her kindly. "They may be getting charged with crimes, or might be bleeding to death on some floor—it just smells rotten for something like this to happen right before we come to court. I need to see them to review their testimony, or to be able to tell you what's going on if they can't make it." Teresa hesitated and swallowed. "I'm only asking for what the law provides." She searched for the telling phrase, the gloss of righteousness intermingled with legal precision that would carry the day, but could muster only, "The Warden knows I came to see you."

The judge stroked his chin. "Tell you what," he finally said. "Let me call the Warden. Come on in."

Teresa followed the Judge into an office that differed from the warden's only by walls that were lined from floor to ceiling with maroon and gold volumes of California law. The judge closed the door behind them, and sat at his desk. Teresa admired his full head of white hair fluffed all the way up and out, a head so striking it made his appointment to the bench as inevitable as night following day.

"Nancy, will you call Lagrimas and get Warden Clayborne on the phone? Thank you."

The two sat silently for a moment.

"How've you been?" the judge asked. She had appeared before him twice, once successfully. His questions about each case made it clear he had not bothered to read any of the papers filed, but he was unfailingly solicitous.

"Right now I can't remember," she answered. If he asked her another such question she was afraid of bursting into tears. The phone rang.

"Okay, put him on." The judge held the phone and waited.

"Hello Warden. Judge Pedrocelli. Teresa Suchil is here, and wants to see her clients today. She says there's been a fight, and one of 'em's hurt. . . . I understand. 9:00? That sounds reasonable. Here's what I'm gonna do. I'll sign an Order requiring you to let her in tomorrow at 9:00. Don't hang her up, now, I don't want any more trouble than what comes naturally. Thank you very much."

The judge hung up the phone and turned to Teresa. "Ms. Suchil, that's the best I can do. If you'll prepare the order—oh, you already have. Well, good luck. Now if you'll excuse me. . . ."

Community Hospital was an ancient building by California standards, one of a very few made of yellow brick. It endured in Grapevine's central core, an area largely torn down in hopeful anticipation of freeways and malls that never materialized, and otherwise abandoned to dark-skinned people, derelicts and bureaucrats in a rush to the northern suburbs.

The hospital consisted of a long trunk joined by one shorter wing. A modern doctor's building joined the hospital's second floor by a glass pedestrian tube that reached over a side street. Teresa entered through the front door, and approached the reception desk.

"Can I help you?" The receptionist was sturdy, short-haired, indifferent.

"Yes. I'm an attorney." Teresa presented one of her cards. "I represent Sergio Magon, one of the Lagrimas inmates brought here this morning." The receptionist stared blankly. "I need to see him. He's a witness in a trial downtown on Monday, and his family is very concerned about him."

"Well. . ."

"I don't want to interfere in any way with his medical treatment. If I could just get a glimpse of him, and talk with one of the treating physicians, it would mean a lot to his family, and enable me to talk with personal knowledge if I have to ask the court for a delay."

The receptionist hesitated, and stopped chewing her gum. "I don't know if we let visitors go into the lockup units."

"I understand. As Mr. Magon's attorney, I'm allowed to see him in prison, jail, anywhere. If he is here for any significant length of time—and our trial is in three days, so *any* time is significant—then I need to see him here, right away."

"Let me talk to someone else." The receptionist telephoned; an older nurse appeared. Teresa repeated her story, and quelled a wave of disgust at the insistence that was such a large part of her work. Complain, beg, wheedle, threaten . . . The nurse reviewed the card entries and said, "I'll have to call the lockup unit and find out where he is. It will be a few minutes."

Teresa turned to the lobby and surveyed the large room in search of a newsstand. A man emerged from the left side of what appeared to be the main corridor and walked slowly past the reception area. He was the same height as Teresa, and his skin was the same burnished copper hue. He was dressed in blue jeans and a guayabera shirt. Beneath his left eye, three dangling teardrops that would never fall were tattooed. Hackles rose on the back of her neck. Teresa blinked; he was gone, and so was her weariness and uncertainty.

"Ms. Suchil, as far as I can tell he is either being operated on or is in the recovery room. Lockup doesn't expect him back until early this evening."

"I'm going to make a phone call and then come back and wait right here until I see my client. I do hope I can see him before too much time passes." The nurse looked closely at her. Teresa was transfixed by the nurse's blue eyes, hemmed in by make-up, like jewels set in brooches. The nurse turned to the telephone.

"Unit 6 Lockup? This is the front desk. You still have a waiting area for visitors?. . . .I know it's not visiting hours. Sergio Magon is apparently due to testify in court next week and his attorney is here. His family is very concerned. . . . She's aware of that. She wants to see him as soon as possible, and is willing to wait outside. . . . Okay, I'll send her up."

The nurse explained how to find the lockup unit. Teresa squeezed the nurse's right hand with both of her own, thanked her profusely, and went to the pay telephone across the lobby.

20

ART ANSWERED THE PHONE. SHE TOLD HIM ALL SHE KNEW OF WHAT had happened in Lagrimas. He whistled. "Jesus fuck, where are you now?"

"In the hospital. I'm staying here until I see Sergio." Teresa gave him the phone number, and added, "Not long ago, while I was standing at the front desk I saw a man with three teardrops tattooed under his left eye, the very man I once met in Folsom prison, remember?"

"I remember."

"What do you know about him?"

Art paused. "Might be Chino Cantu. He's one of the founders of the Vida Loca—but they got no reason to come after us. I thought he was in Folsom, anyway."

"Why don't you call Aaron—he's got the official name and number of everyone I ever visited—and have him check with the Records Office. And please have someone by the phone all day and night."

"All right, Terry. You be careful, now."

"Same to you all, you're not on the other side of the world, you know." They hung up their phones together, strained by their new burden of politeness.

A central staircase to the third floor led to a nurse's station and waiting area positioned where the wing met the central corridor. Three yellow plastic chairs, a short couch and two small tables holding well-thumbed

magazines were scattered about the nurse's area. A closed steel door to
the wing behind the nurse's station blocked all traffic that did not
announce itself to a squawkbox and put proper papers in a slot. One chair
squarely opposite the nurse's desk afforded views up and down the long
corridor.

Teresa introduced herself to the nurse on duty. "Mr. Magon's
operation will be a long one, and he'll be in the recovery room a while
after that," she informed Teresa. "We don't expect him back until
sometime late tonight."

"I'll wait. Where are the elevators?"

"There's one at each end of the corridor."

"The operating room and the recovery room?"

"Both are on the second floor, toward that end." The nurse gestured
over her shoulder.

"Did you happen to see a man in blue jeans about my height, medium
build, who had teardrops tattooed under one eye?"

"No, no one like that. I'm sure I'd notice."

Teresa walked to one end of the main corridor, looked through the
glass wall and hazy air over a parking lot to downtown Grapevine. The
heavy door and squawkbox made it unlikely that anyone could push
through to the Lockup ward from the outside—but who was waiting
inside? A rumbling noise and a blast of cold air on her back stopped
simultaneously as the air conditioner switched off. Voices echoed more
loudly than they should in a hospital, she thought; but I'm hypersensitive.
Teresa felt like a deer as she walked slowly to the other end of the
corridor, alert for the presence of predators.

Corridor traffic seemed light. She passed three briskly stepping staff
members, nurses gathered at the nurse station, and two older patients in
no hurry to reach their destination. Most doors were closed. As she
approached the end an elevator opened and two deputy sheriffs
emerged, each holding the arm of a young man wearing a bright orange
jumpsuit. The young man whistled at her, and was yanked past by the
deputies. The glass wall at the other end of the corridor looked over the
top of a tunnel that led from the medical office building across the street.

She rode the elevator down to the second floor, and walked its length
and down the wing as well, which was accessible through swinging doors.
People moved in all directions, on tables, in chairs or on their own two

feet. A tang of medicinal odors and disinfectants mingled with the smells of nervous sweat and fear pheromes that seeped out of the inhabitants and hung in the air in spite of the intermittent cold breeze.

As she approached the operating room, she saw a patient on an operating table being slowly moved down the hall by two nurses. Each pushed the table with one hand and with the other pushed a metal tree on a wheeled tripod base that held plastic bags and bottles of fluids connected to the patient with plastic tubes. The unwieldy procession moved at a stately pace. Its creaking, squeaking rasp of metal joints and ten wheels rolling on linoleum and the shuffle of four guiding feet blended into a unique harmony, the sound Sergio would make when he emerged from the operating room.

Teresa left the hospital to fetch her coat and books from the car. The afternoon heat was ferocious; her tolerance for it had dissipated as she lived with the coastal fogs. When she returned, she stationed herself in the chair closest to the main corridor, and began to wait. The slightest head move enabled her to see down the corridor to the elevator that would bring Sergio up from the recovery room. The light was bright neon, the kind that seemed designed to highlight skin eruptions and other flaws. Its effect on the flesh of patients in particular was most unhappy.

Deputy sheriffs occasionally entered and left the closed wing, escorting patients together with a nurse when the patient was laid out, or in pairs when moving ambulatory men.

The day shift of nurses left, the swing shift came. At the moment of transition, Teresa approached the desk; recognition transferred. She read magazines and looked occasionally up and down the long hall. Stainless steel food carts rolled past. The window behind her became a forbidding rectangular glare of light; the next time she looked it glowed a soft red that merged with its reflection on the floor. She rose and walked down the hall to watch the sunset.

The smoggy Grapevine air turned a lovely violet, and the sun became a bright red ball while still high above the horizon. Cars drove by, some with lights on, all without a sound, on the street below. The sun slid down behind the buildings of downtown Grapevine like a slowly flattening balloon. The evening finally became black, and the window reflected her face and the corridor behind her.

Teresa went downstairs and traded all her loose change for a batch of stale food. She returned to her station and learned from the nurse that she had missed nothing. She ate her food and consumed all the unread prose within reach. Her alertness leaked slowly out and was swept away by the air blower. Teresa put on her tweed jacket, and waited and waited, past all sense of time moving. Eventually, her eyes shaded by her straw hat, she fell into a fitful sleep.

She woke to the same fishbelly hospital light and saw, over the bunched folds of her white hospital gown and the bare high mound of her stomach, six young males, talking, staring at her, laughing! Her secret heart, a place coveted by many, reached by a very few awestruck exemplars, now casually pointed out and poked at by random monsters somehow licensed to abuse her because she was about to give birth, to continue the human race. They responded to her bulging eyes with curt nods as if she were a fellow intern seen on a downtown street, and babbled incomprehensible sounds that dissolved into braying laughter every 60 seconds like a demented metronome, and she could neither move nor scream.

Pricked awake by the immobility of her dream, Teresa opened her eyes. Nothing moved other than a nurse making file entries at her desk. The bright light pressed her eyes shut again.

She stood against the wall of another hospital, this time in a green gown instead of white. Intense young men and curious older men came to talk at her. They chattered awhile, and went away. She thought of eating, of asking about her child, but could not see the point of either. She focused on the repetitive dark and light green geometric patterns on the floor. A man operating a machine-driven brush that whirled and polished the floor approached. He talked to her and ran his machine near her feet. When she could feel the machine's wind she left her wall for a moment, just long enough for her spot to be polished, and then stood again next to the wall until the lights came on. The light above was pushy, almost ugly enough to uproot her, but if she moved from her spot, where would she go? Her hospital room, her husband's apartment, her parents' house, the unknown, nothing was *vale la pena*. Staying put was best. She did not care to either move or scream.

The sounds of another changing shift awoke her. She exchanged greetings and made explanatory murmurings, and settled back into her chair. The light around the nurse's station had not changed, but the long hall was now dim.

The dark man was after her. He had chased her through her dreams in the night for twenty years, mostly up and down fire escapes, bridge pylons, water tanks, and stairwells of a city she did not know. She had tried to escape in subway stations, on electric buses and streetcars and in elevator shafts, and she ran, sometimes so fast on winged feet that she left the ground and soared; other times she felt mired waist-deep in cool honey, her most strenuous exertions barely raised one leg, and she allowed exhaustion to take her over and make her curious as to what her fate would be if she waited for him. He had never reached her. Now, he was chasing her through the neat suburban streets of north Fresno, the neighborhood of her father's dreams. It seemed hard to believe that the dark man could find that area of split-level homes, swing sets, and flowering bushes bordering clipped lawns where her mother had lost herself somewhere between the Master Bedroom, Family Room and Den, but he was coming through the ghosts of uprooted fig trees and vineyards, darting from behind a Plymouth's tail fins to the last living relic of the central valley's life before development, a gargantuan, twisted oak tree, only one back yard away, closer than ever before. A branch of the oak reached out to her bedroom window and scratched it with stiff winter twigs, trying to push it open.

The scratching, squeaking sound her ears were attuned to receive awoke her. She blinked her eyes, and peered down the corridor. A cart moved slowly toward her between two metal trees. A deputy sheriff and a nurse each had a hand on the cart and on one of the trees, pushing them forward. A shadowy figure crossed the hall behind them, in front of the farthest hall light.

Teresa stood up and walked into the hall. The shadow came quickly, silently toward the three figures inching forward in the center of the hall. Glints of light sparked from his face.

"Look out behind you!" she screamed.

The deputy and the nurse lifted their heads and looked at her. Teresa pointed her finger, screamed again, "He's coming toward you!" and ran down the hall to the cart. The deputy turned around slowly, reluctant to take his eyes off Teresa. When he saw the man coming he yelled "Watch out, Anna!" and ran forward toward Teresa and past her. The nurse never turned, but when she saw the deputy break from the cart she took a deep breath and lunged forward with him on past Teresa, who reached the cart together with a dark man wearing reflector glasses.

His arm wheeled high and came down flashing. Teresa jerked the cart toward her and to the right, knocking over one of the metal trees. The knife in the man's hand entered the left hip of the body on the cart. Plastic tubes dripped and waved free like vines in a storm as Teresa lunged for the wrist above the knife and grabbed it with both hands.

The man smashed her face with his left hand and she slumped to the floor holding on as tight as if she were clinging to a guard rail on the edge of a cliff.

Chino was barely able to wrench the knife loose and keep his feet. The woman clinging to his wrist was tangled in a metal tree. He hit her again, very hard, and felt her face give way. Her grip loosened slightly. He hesitated between hitting her a third time in the face, hacking her wrist with the edge of his free palm or reaching down with his left hand to remove the knife from his right, and barely had time to block the descending arc of the deputy's black club with his forearm. Weighted with lead, the club struck his arm with tremendous force, smashing the smaller bone. The deputy lifted his club again, and a surge of adrenalin powered Chino's right hand free and sent him over to the other side of the cart.

The deputy's club wavered high in the air. The body on the cart bled profusely. The nurse's mouth pressed a telephone. Other deputies waited in the closed wing, with firearms. Chino decided to run.

Deputy Walsh, pleased and surprised that he had swung his club with such effect, ran toward the fleeing figure and yelled, "Stop, you son of a bitch!" The dark man disappeared down the staircase. For the first time a wave of fear passed through the deputy, and he shuddered violently.

When the doctors and nurses and deputies arrived, they saw the deputy trembling, and a bloody Teresa gasping for air like a fish yanked from water as she slumped over the body on the cart. The only calm person present was Sergio Magon. Heavily sedated, his nerves severed that connected his lower body sensations to his brain, he was unaware of the blood flowing from his thigh. Sergio was nine years old again and working in a vineyard. Assigned to rid the grapevines of pests, he lay on his back in the dirt under the shade of broad translucent leaves, looking up at bugs moving across the delicate green veins with what appeared to be a great purpose. As he was reconnected to his tubes and wheeled back toward the elevator, he heard the caw of a crow and thought, What a pity to disturb any of God's creatures on such a hot afternoon.

21

CALIFORNIA'S CENTRAL VALLEY IS AN ELONGATED BOWL 20 TO 50 MILES wide and 400 miles long that spills west into the Pacific Ocean. Thousands of streams pour down from the surrounding mountains into the valley's two rivers, the Sacramento in the north and the San Joaquin in the south. The rivers merge in a marshy delta and then squeeze through the Carquinez Straits into the San Francisco Bay and the ocean beyond.

The valley's flat bottom is deep loam soil. Rains from the ocean blow in over the coastal hills and drench the valley from November through March. The high wall of the Sierra Nevada catches and holds the rain in a deep snowpack, and releases it gradually when hit by the constant summer sun.

Dams built all around the valley's edge since the late 19th century block winter floods, drain lakes, provide the exact amount of water desired on schedule, and supply abundant amounts of the cheapest form of electrical power. Intensive investments of capital and labor produce enormous, predictable harvests of money and a feudal social structure more hierarchical than in the nearby foothills and more rigid than in the coastal cities. Continually stoked with mountain water and groundwater and fertilizers and pesticides and driven without rest to produce billions of dollars worth of food for export to all parts of the world, the valley is destined to become an exhausted sandpit sucked dry of nutrients, poisoned with salts and polychlorinated hydrocarbons, depreciated for tax purposes, and abandoned like a used-up mineshaft by the restless money that once spent itself so freely. A shitbrindled haze now usually swallows the horizons. Except for a few tantalizing hours after the clearing of a winter storm, when jagged peaks to the east and curving hills to the west delineate boundaries, the valley's essential nature is hidden, available only in stories or books.

A menace of haze and smoke hung in the air like flammable gas as Raphael Matus drove across the valley floor toward Grapevine. Robert Chime accompanied him as he drove. They sat silently for two hours while Raphael thought about what lay ahead, but his mind eventually wore ruts through the same set of facts and rubbed itself raw against the same dangerous conclusions. He wanted to talk.

Robert slouched against the door like a sack of rice, but his eyes were restless and brilliant, the eyes of a newly caged animal. Raphael asked him questions about how he was doing, and was answered by random grunts. He reached over and touched Robert's shoulder.

"Hey Robert."

"Yes?"

"Dostoyevsky said, 'The degree of civilization in a society can be judged by entering its prisons.' Do you know why he was right?"

"No." The word crackled.

"Because there you find the bottom of the social order. What's a person entitled to simply because he's human? Light? Air? Food? Bodily movement? How much? Contact with others? Family, friends, political associates? By mail or in the flesh? Movies, radio? Who decides? What appeal? Huh?" He reached out and nudged Robert, who retreated further into the door. "These questions are answered every day in prison.

"It hasn't always been this way. Forty years ago the farthest edge of humanity wasn't found in prisons, but nuthouses. Prisons were thought to be filled with regular dudes played by Jimmy Cagney, guys who happened to take a wrong turn. Insane asylums were different: huge spooky places way out in the woods behind high walls, full of eerie moans, gibbering idiots, mad scientists packing long gold needles. . . .

"Nowadays, it's turned around. Most people above the lower classes have been to a shrink or know someone who was or is or ought to be in therapy. The business of nervous breakdowns is familiar, an old story - but prisons are different. The new myth is that they are filled with evil beasts of some other species than human, a myth that allows endless abuse."

Robert stared vacantly out the closed side window at a cluster of trucks huddled under a tall sign that flashed a purple berry pie slice and the words "24 hr." He turned to look at Raphael when the words stopped, and saw a remote carved mahogany deity sitting still at the wheel. The tops of long truck trailers whooshed toward them over oleander bushes in full pink and white bloom, fume-eating flowers that divided the highway.

Robert washed every dinner dish in a deep steel sink. The water was scalding hot. It thickened with grease as he whipped through the dishes, glasses, and silverware brought to him by the table-cleaners. He refilled the sink twice, plunging his arm deep into the water to pull the plug. Dryers took rinsed dishes from him, dried them, and ran them over to the resort cabinets. People swept to and fro around him, as he washed, rinsed, and stacked with ever greater efficiency and speed. Finally, he wrestled with big blackened encrusted pots, and scoured them clean. "Anything else?" he yelled. After waiting a decent interval and hearing no reply, Robert dashed out of the kitchen into the night.

A half moon supplied enough light for him to find his way across the grass to his cabin for a shower, then back up the canyon to the stairs of the bath-house that contained the round steel tub.

He opened the door and peered in. The room was very dark; light came from flickering candles and a hole in the roof. Faces flickered through billowing coils of steam that rose continuously from the tub in the center of the room. As he squinted to see who was in the tub, Teresa said, "Hi, Robert." He walked quickly over the slatted floor, added his clothes to a pile on one of the benches, groped his way to the tub's edge, and climbed in. "Hi," he sighed, and drifted down until his eyes were just above the surface.

He was in an immense, steaming cauldron, a lake reflecting the light of the moon. Toes tickled his feet. Rita Valdez talked quietly to Teresa. Tyrone's dark mountain shape was silhouetted by an opening in the wall behind that led to a shallow pool on a terrace above individual bath cabins. Robert could hear Art and Myrna giggling and splashing just outside, and Raphael talking on the stairs.

Aaron must still be with the old man, he thought, and remembered the icy shock of the creek pool into which he had leapt that afternoon while walking with Aaron and the man who owned the resort. Robert felt himself dissolve like a cube of sugar between the memory of ice and the presence of fire, and sat up straight. People were climbing in from all sides; Aaron had joined them. His shoulder was used as a brace. When the splash and clatter died down, everyone was in the tub.

Jokes, insults, remarks faded, and were replaced by "oooo's" of appreciation. Robert stayed low in the water, and looked at the bodies around him. The lighter ones glowed like embers. The darker ones glittered as water dropped from hair, ran down shoulders and spilled from the hollow cavities of collarbones. Teresa's curls were so stubborn that they twisted even when dripping wet. Robert looked and looked, and listened with half an ear to the conversation until a woozy reminder of food and wine overcame him. It passed as he sat up, but he decided to get some air.

He rolled over, grasped the side of the tub, and pulled himself up. As he stood, those on each side of him moved together. He was left standing near the tub's middle.

"Heeey, Robert!"

"Lookin' mighty good!"

"Oooo, what a cutie!"

"I think he'll do," said Myrna. "I'll take half a dozen."

Robert stayed in the middle of the tub, and made a slow turn.

"Oww, check him out!"

"Heartbreaker!"

The hoots and raillery increased. Just as the rising volume leveled off, Robert lifted his arms above his head, gave a sharp pelvic bump, and scrambled out of the tub and down the stairs, leaving squeals of delight in his wake.

Robert broke into a very wide smile and thought, Not bad for a virgin. The dry air had cooled quickly once the sun went down, but he felt naked and invincible, as self-contained as the dolphins who roam the oceans from the Equator to the Poles without ever donning or shedding clothes.

The tepid water of the swimming pool was a mild shock quickly dissipated by kicks and long strokes that carried him back and forth through the water until his arms began to feel heavy and his legs and head lost their coordination. He dried himself with a towel thrown over a nearby chair and lay down to rest.

He dozed, and woke up shivering. The moon was down. He stumbled to the tub room and put on his clothes. From the top of the porch he heard faint voices on the hill above the cabins, and saw a dim glow. He fetched his flashlight and found his way toward a clearing, centered by a campfire. Around the fire were Art, Myrna, and Teresa. They bade him sit down on a log. The fire shaped a cozy room out of the night.

"Well, everybody's gone to bed but us," yawned Myrna.

"That's the way it is," brooded Art, "and that's the way it'll stay. We're the ones who will do the job, or it won't get done. Raphael and Aaron and Tyrone all have career tracks they're ridin'. They add tone to the organization. We need 'em to succeed. The fact is, though, they're day trippers. When the phone rings, or the thief with twenty hot watches and an electric typewriter comes around, or one of the retired teamsters who lives in the bar across the street gets feisty, or the fuses blow out or the roof leaks, it's on us to take care of it."

The wind and the flames died down; Art stared into the fire's embers. "Terry, let me tell you something about them convicts. Most of 'em are a low-life bunch of chickenshit snivelers, always wantin' somethin' for nothin'. Lots of 'em are gettin' turned out as snitches, somethin' that just wasn't *done* when I was in the pen."

"Oh, Art—"

"—Now Myrna here likes 'em—she even married one, somethin' I sure as hell wouldn't do. They're gonna talk Union talk to you because they want to be your pen pal, and get another look at your body and get you involved in whatever swamp of a case they're stuck in. People ready to ride their own beefs and organize the Union are gonna be few and far between."

"I think I can be clear that the reason I'm driving all the way to prison is to work with people interested in the Union. If anyone insists on talking about . . ."

"Ahhh, you'll run into a lot of slick bullshit from people whose only interest is in getting you to come back—if it took a knowledge of algebra to do it, they'd jam all night with math books before the visit, rattle off equations while they were with you, and use the books for toilet paper after trading their issue for cigarettes."

"Art! Surely somebody who's locked up wants a union both inside and outside the prison. I've read enough mail—"

"Of course! They all would! But nobody wants to get stranded out on front street for something that ain't likely to happen, that the smart money isn't backing. So, they'll try to derail you onto the monstrous injustice that landed their own ass in the joint even though they were caught dead and stinkin', and already confessed! They'll tell you that a victory in their case would have great implications"—Art spread his arms wide, dropping Myrna's head into his lap—"for the criminal justice system, that they're willing to Serve the People by crusading with you on their case. Hey, I know how those sleazebuckets think, Terry, I lived with 'em for the better part of the last twenty years."

Myrna seemed asleep, curled up next to Art. He looked down at her for a moment, and kissed her on the forehead. "Most convicts think they're irresistible to women, even though they've never gotten anything in their lives they didn't either rip off or pay cash up front for. You know, if we fall on our ass, every convict will say they knew this half-assed, harebrained idea never had a chance; that Art Simpson always had his head up his ass, Tyrone just wanted some stoop labor, and Raphael stayed in school too long. If we ever get this thing goin', though, if we really do it, get some justice and *equity* inside the penitentiary, every last convict will claim it was his unappreciated hard work and bright ideas that made it all possible, and we're all ungrateful dogs for not givin' him the credit."

Art gave Myrna a squeeze. She stirred. "C'mon, sweetie," he said, "let's go to bed."

Myrna stood up, and stretched. "Terry, we're really happy to have you. Once you learn how to ignore Art when he flaps his mouth, I think you'll like it working for the Union."

"Hey, no kiddin', Terry, I'm thrilled fuckin' silly to have you. We've got to have a lawyer—nobody else can get inside to see our members, nobody else can talk to a damn judge." Art shook his head as he stood. "You can't go to the bathroom these days without an attorney to hold your hand."

He stepped over to Teresa and looked at her closely. "We need somebody to sue the prison system for our right to meet inside," he said. "We won't be a real union until we do. Hell, the alcoholics and the Catholics, and now the Brotherhood, get to meet inside. Why can't we? We've done a lot less harm than any of *them*.

"I've badgered every lawyer I can think of to do us a lawsuit on our members' right to meet in the same way other groups meet, with us bein' the outside sponsors, but nobody will do it. Oh, they'll fuck around with our mail and the newspaper, but nobody will get up to the table and ask for the main course."

Teresa extended her hand to Art and said firmly, "Well, I'll do it. The court can't say anything worse than No, right?"

Art took her hand with both of his as Myrna doused the fire. "You know, the only reason I ran all that stuff is that I'm so glad to have you I'm scared to death that you'll make one visit to prison, meet six lops and lames instead of Malcolm X or some hero, say, Who needs this shit, and leave."

Teresa laughed a ringing, bell-toned laugh. "Here I am, Art, way out in the woods. You've got me . . ."

Raphael was talking about first principles, the meaning of 'civil dead', and 'union', the origin of names. Robert had yearned to hear such talk a year earlier, but now the words rattled inside the vehicle like loose pieces of metal.

"We don't want to define what kind of union we are too precisely," Raphael concluded. "It would only diminish us."

"Sounds pretty goddamn sneaky to me," said Robert.

"Sneaky?!" Raphael sat up in the driver's seat as if he had been poked with a sharp stick, glad for the stimulation. "There's a serious difference between ambiguous and sneaky. We want to evoke an array of responses, not deceive. We're not working for farm laborers who pick the lettuce we eat in our salads, or any other group you can drum up support for just by prodding people into remembering connections they like to forget. Prisoners are the most despised members of society. We're running straight up against deep hatreds that churn around beneath the surface of rational discourse, and we can't afford to be slovenly about something as important as a name."

"Did you make the whole thing up?" Robert's voice was unexpectedly loud.

"What?"

"Are we all actors in some movie you're producing and directing?"

"No," Raphael answered, after a moment's thought. "The Union arose out of everybody's circumstances, including my own. It just happened." He grinned. "Part of my job is to make up reasons after the fact for whatever we decide to do."

Robert felt a clinging urge to smash him. Instead, he turned to look out their window at the highway life that was washing over and past in rhythmic time, and lulled himself into calmness.

"Ms. Suchil is in Room 343. She has several visitors."

"We won't be long," said Raphael.

After talking with a deputy at the third floor nurses' station, they found Teresa's room. An old man in the bed nearest the door greeted them with a wrenching cough.

Teresa was on the window side of a double room divided by a partition, propped up against three pillows, staring through two black cracked saucers around her eyes that were separated by a white vertical line of steel-reinforced gauze covering her nose. Her bandaged hands lay next to each other on her covers, and a young girl lay beside her, head buried where the pillows met the sheet, arm over her mother, apparently asleep. Art and Myrna sat in the room's two chairs. Robert touched her lightly, afraid to squeeze, and moved back to the window.

"Teresa, you know who hit you?" Raphael asked quietly.

She nodded.

"Was it the man you described to Art on the phone, the man with teardrops under his eyes?"

She nodded quickly, before he finished his sentence.

"Have you talked to the police?"

"She just woke up. They'll be back," said Myrna, looking at her watch, "any minute now."

"Would you mind waiting a while before saying anything about the teardrops?"

Teresa looked him in the eye for a moment, and then shook her head.

"Good. I'll be back later to talk." Raphael gestured to Art, who rose and accompanied him to the cafeteria in the hospital's basement.

"How's she doing?"

"Broken nose, not too hard to reset, lost a tooth. Had a concussion; they're gonna watch her for a couple of days."

"Magon?"

"Dead and gone. Helluva goddamn ad for the Union, eh?—join the Union and get stuck like a fuckin' pincushion." Art sipped his coffee gingerly, as if it were nitroglycerine.

"Chino was paroled four months ago to Grapevine."

"No shit. Well, why in the fuck would he do a risky, nasty, crazy thing like this?"

"I'm going to Cristo Rey to try and find out."

"Want me to come?"

"No. It's the kind of place where you either send one man or an army. I'll be back here in three hours. If I'm not, find an army and send it. You'll be here in the cafeteria or with Teresa?"

"Right."

Raphael stood to go, but was waved back down to his seat.

"You know what?" growled Art. "The bitch has got me again."

"What do you mean?"

"What do I mean?" Art reached into the empty air and clenched his fist, struggling for the words. "I mean, the bitch has got me again!" He pointed his finger at Raphael. "Listen, man. I'm sick of all the bullshit and bad-mouthing. I don't care about the newspapers or the legislature, I don't care about convicts anymore. I'm tired of doing what I've been doing. I did my time inside, and now I've done my time outside. I've thought a lot about what Teresa said the other night, and you know what? She was dead right."

Raphael had heard several versions of what had come to be called the Bummer Meeting. "There's no more reason to put stock in what either of you said at that meeting than there is to believe a cat in heat."

"Cats in heat screech, but they don't lie," said Art triumphantly. Raphael regretted his sorry choice of metaphor. "I don't care to search out the job of a parole officer, but if it fell on me—" Art shrugged—"Hell, I could stand it. The regular paycheck, nice routine paperwork, keeping the forms filled out, making a few humanitarian gestures at Christmas time, why not? Seein' through convict lies and pullin' 'em up - the fact is, man, I want to quit, resign. The Union needs me to resign.

"I don't know what the hell else I can do with myself. I don't have the stomach for crime anymore, and I've never done anything but be a crook or a convict or an ex-convict and the truth is, I'm scared shitless to find out. I really want to know if there's anything else out there for me, but I'll never find out so long as I'm President of the Union. Two nights ago

I finally gutted up and decided absolutely to resign after our hearing, no looking back. And you know what? After all this shit has come down, I can't do it!"

"Damned right you can't." Raphael spoke quickly. "You'd look like dogshit if you cut out now. We've got to clear this up before you can even think about it."

Art turned his copy of the newspaper toward Raphael, who saw the headline: HOSPITAL ATTACK. "Like I say," Art said with grim satisfaction, "the bitch has got me again."

Raphael drove south from Grapevine on a two-lane road, into the sad agribusiness heart of the valley, thinking about Art and their time together in Soledad prison 20 years earlier. After his conviction for armed robbery Raphael had killed time in Soledad for two years, and then, for reasons no less mysterious to himself than to the professional rehabilitators around him, he suddenly quit smoking and began to eat vitamins, avoid meat, run several miles a day, and lift weights. He also began to read books, and made a list each day of fifteen new words and their definitions.

Art had joined in this strict regimen for the experience, but once having known health he lost interest, and resumed his efforts to gain money and cigarettes by polishing his chess game, crafting model stagecoaches and other paraphernalia of the Old West for hobby-shop visitors, and manufacturing alcoholic drinks in his cell.

Raphael, however, never stopped. His momentum carried him out of prison and through college and graduate school to a tenured position as a full professor of political science. Circumstantial changes did not alter his habit of structuring every minute of his days. The pleasures of unremitting discipline could not be bought off the rack; they were an elixir of an infinite number of small increments so rare and intense that Raphael secretly thought his perfect discipline a shameless indulgence.

He refused to bury the past as do most ex-convicts who seek the rewards of the straight world. Raphael incorporated his prison time into his persona, in order to inspire other convicts and intimidate his academic colleagues who had not Been There.

Art and Tyrone never deigned to notice any changes in him over their two decades with Raphael, and he loved them for it. Art embodied for Raphael those qualities commonly called human: vulnerability, impulsiveness, transparence, weakness in the face of temptation, courage when confronted, a stubborn desperate nerve. Raphael was bound by an implacable bargain with his conscience to work with the Union, in order that he might spend his money with pleasure. He did not want to do so without Art. Fortunately, Art's dissatisfaction had forced its way into consciousness where it could be dealt with. Raphael was ready to reach deep into his pocket of incentives - praise, an offer of steady money, a personal plea; whatever would hook Art into staying.

He turned twice onto smaller roads that led through an unending plantation of summer fruit trees. Ranks and files of nectarine trees pruned into squat dusty chalices crowded both sides of the narrow road. Occasional lanes on each side of the roads pointed towards distant oases marked by tall, lean palms. 45 minutes after leaving Grapevine, he bounced over potholes that in lieu of any signs announced the border of Cristo Rey.

Bedraggled citrus trees and dusty palms wavered haphazardly among small, bleached wood houses. He turned left at the blinding glare of the only new building in town, a huge packing shed by the railroad tracks, and followed the tracks to his destination.

Cristo Rey was the kind of town not commonly thought to exist in the United States, and therefore was ignored by governmental officials. Spanish, not English, was the tongue of its residents. The normal channels for spirit and matter regarded as vital in other towns - curbs for the streets, schools for the children, police for the lawbreakers - didn't exist. Law enforcement was provided by deputy sheriffs from faraway Grapevine, who occasionally rode into town in a pack of never less than five vehicles and rousted everyone in the bars that lined the railroad tracks along Main Street.

Raphael parked his car in an empty lot of hard dirt next to the largest bar in town. The bar would be immediately recognized by anyone who has served the United States' empire in Vietnam or Okinawa or South Korea or the Philippines. A bevy of dark, very short miniskirted young women caked with layers of pale make-up idled in the shade around wide open bar doors waiting for the night.

It was late afternoon, a slow time of day in a slow season, after the harvest and before the pruning. A poster in the club's only window advised its readers to Reelect Sheriff Cheney. Ceiling fans pushed sweat and flies slowly across the faces of more women in miniskirts inside the bar as they played pool or lolled about watching the balls bounce. An anonymous synthetic beat pulsed, wildly out of time with the languid movements of those in the bar. Above the empty dance floor and bandstand a mirrored globe slowly swirled; rectangles of light turned in circles on the floor beneath.

The bar was in the farthest corner, by the restrooms and what may have been the office. Raphael approached the office slowly. He did not care to surprise anybody. The club might look sluggish, but it supplied the two corporations that owned the surrounding land with labor from Mexico, distributed drugs for resale up and down the Central Valley, and siphoned off a considerable percentage of the wages of workers who lived in holes and shacks behind the fruit trees. It did several million dollars worth of business a year, and Raphael assumed that its owners would not leave it untended.

An older woman with stiff curled hair the color of black shoe polish emerged from the shadows of the office.

"Good afternoon," he said in Spanish.

"What do you want?" Her question was devoid of curiosity.

"I would like to talk with Chino Cantu."

The woman exhibited no trace of recognition. She glanced over her shoulder at the shadows, and finally said, "He's not here."

Rafael extended his card to her. "Five people know where he was last night. Tell him I want to reach an understanding with him, before anybody else finds out."

The woman took his card, and studied it as if she were looking for ant tracks. "Just a minute," she said, and turned to go back to the office. Her neck craned slightly as she reached the office door, and he felt Chino's presence close at hand.

Rafael drifted toward the bar as nonchalantly as he could, and waited. Half an hour passed before the woman returned. She was more animated; a ripple of cautious anger crossed her face.

"He has left the area, and will not be back soon. It was an unfortunate mistake. The one who caused it is a traitor inside the penitentiary. He will be handled. Chino says to tell you he is sorry."

Her eyes were flat, glazed with finality. The pounding rhythm abruptly stopped, and the Five Satins began crooning "In the Still of the Night."

"Tell him that I very much want to talk with him. He can call me anytime, from anywhere." Rafael's back tingled as he walked slowly out of the bar, and did not settle down until he was halfway to Grapevine.

22

Teresa awoke alone in a sunlit hospital room filled with flowers. Her bound hands tingled, and her face throbbed with knocks of muffled pain.

A nurse suddenly appeared from around a partition, and told Teresa she was "just forty feet down the hall from where that man attacked you. Convenient, I must say.

"You look perfectly horrible, dear. I tell you only so you won't drop this valuable 49-cent mirror we provide our better patients." The nurse set the mirror on Teresa's bedside table and handed her a glass of water and two pills. "Here, take these right now."

Teresa swallowed the pills and ignored the mirror. "Were you here—"

"Yes, we talked yesterday. You don't remember? You don't remember." The nurse bustled about Teresa's bed, fluffing pillows.

"What did you say?" The nurse told her that Mr. Magon died a few hours after he was stabbed, that he would have probably died anyway from the first round of stab wounds, and that her doctor would come to see her. Teresa sank deeper into her bed. Tears began to flow of their own accord, almost casually, detached from any feeling.

The nurse continued to talk. "Joann Reilly from the Daily News is here right now insisting that you will be overjoyed to see her. I told her not—"

"Joann!" Pain shot from Teresa's jaw across her face. "Please," she said quietly, searching for a register and cadence that would be less assaultive, "send her in."

"Terry, what a god-awful way to meet!" Joann kissed Teresa's forehead. "I'm sorry, so sorry."

"Mmmmph," Teresa said quietly through her teeth. Joann showed her a newspaper headlined HOSPITAL ATTACK. "I told my boss we were best friends in high school, and got assigned to cover the story. A little embroidery, but I *really* wanted the assignment."

"Is Sergio Magon really dead?"

"Yes."

"Did they catch the man who stabbed him?"

"No, he got away through the office building across the street. No one has any idea who he was. They'll get him, though—every cop in the state is after him. There's a deputy here at the desk 'round the clock. You want to read my stories?"

"Not now." Teresa tried to focus on Joann's face, but it was too slippery. Her tears continued on their own path, while Teresa calculated. She had not seen Joann over the last decade, and did not know who she had become. Joann had never seemed cynical or all-knowing enough to be a newspaper person, but had done well. "Who have you talked to?" she asked.

"Your friends from the Union. They've been nice enough, but vague. My main source has been James Orr, the prison flak. He speculates that it's a drug-related gang fight, but has nothing definite to say."

"What happened in the prison?"

"Two dead. Two here in Community. One will probably be charged with two counts of murder."

"Who?"

"Frederick Carlyle Johnson."

Teresa felt a distant shudder. "Any ideas on why it happened, or how word got out from the prison about where Magon was? The whole place was locked down at 9:30 in the morning when I arrived."

"No. As a matter of fact I asked Orr directly, too, and he slid around it with some blather. . . ."

The two women were quiet for a moment. A maxim floated up from Teresa's days of collecting words to live by: If you want to find out if a person is trustworthy, trust her.

"Joann, do you have husbands or children or other trappings?"

"I have half a duplex in Fig Orchard with mother in the other half."

"Do you have room for me wherever you're living? Just for a while. I might be kinda hot . . ."

"Of course I do, I'd love to have you around. You know who it was, don't you. The person who attacked you."

Teresa lifted her bound hands, and dropped them hard enough to sting. "Let's nail this down, okay?"

Joann leaned down, squeezed Teresa's arm, whispered "Okay" in her ear, and quietly left the room.

Everyone from the Union came to see her. The police came, and she told them all she could remember except her sighting of the man with tattooed teardrops in the afternoon. Finally, the nurse cleared the room. Teresa was under orders to do nothing.

She woke in the middle of the night, and reached over to the nightstand for a glass of water. None was there, but a blaring newspaper headline atop a stack of papers drew her attention. It concerned an assault on her. She reached for it; her dreams had been so dense and vivid that her sense of what had really happened was blurred, and chronological order lost.

Joann's initial story recounted the night's violence and how its perpetrator had escaped from the hospital. There was a photograph of Teresa taken during a speaking engagement in Grapevine three months earlier, and a picture of the deputy who had chased the assailant away, taken in the heat of the moment. The story detailed the results of the morning's violence at the prison. Two short paragraphs talked of the lawsuit and hearing, postponed by the court on its own order.

The lawsuit. Teresa no longer cared about doing the hearing. The realization shocked her; she checked again. Not a trace of her desire remained. The lawsuit would be a chore, like taking out the garbage. What had happened?

"If the Sun and Moon would Doubt, they'd immediately Go Out. . . ." She was very thirsty. Repeated pushes of the Help button finally prodded a nurse into coming, and she asked for a glass of water.

She still supported the values embodied in the lawsuit, but they had moved from her center to the far edges of her being. Teresa was alarmed that such sea changes could happen without her presence. How else had she changed? Did she still know her own mind? Had she ever? Her landscape of values felt no different, but she had been punched from one quadrant to another. A brief effort to rekindle her enthusiasm felt like blowing into the mouth of a corpse. Anger against this unexpected toll of violence changed nothing.

When she thought of the Union as she lay in her hospital bed, she did not think of due process of law or any of the principles that had so impressed her with how they arched across centuries and continents; she saw images of Myrna working steadily at her desk, Art talking to two people at once— How could she have let herself be so cruel to Art, so oblivious to Myrna? An image of Robert's smooth skin shifted to Fred Johnson curled in the corner of an empty cell, his body swollen and bruised, and her mind finally turned to the picture nibbling at its corners, of Sergio Magon being stabbed. It stayed there as he was stabbed again and again and again. Efforts to invoke other pictures failed; her consciousness clung to the image of a thrusting knife, a clock pendulum swinging back and forth, back and forth.

She lunged blindly for the button that would bring a nurse with narcotics and patted the wall until she grazed the button with her palm. When she found it she held her hand just above the button and did not push. Then, the image shifted, and she lay back to join Sergio across a table for a long visit in which they traded biographical details and marveled at the similarities in their seemingly different lives. It was a relaxed conversation between two people who have all the time in the world, and nothing better to do than talk with each other.

Teresa called the prison from her bed once she knew the date she was leaving the hospital and made appointments to see the Fly and Fred Johnson the following day. She was told that David Carruthers had been moved to a Los Angeles County Work Furlough Center. The hearing, postponed until August 30, had sprung back to the center of her concerns. She remained stuck at the angle from which she had seen it two nights earlier, but for the moment she was grateful to it for giving structure to her days and something concrete to think about besides the throb in her face and hands.

The prison remained locked down. When she arrived at the visiting room, she saw no one other than one female guard and another attorney visiting his client. The Fly appeared quickly.

"Let's sit out in the middle," he said upon arriving at her cubicle. "Our odds of avoiding their electronic toys are better."

They sat across from one another in the middle of the visiting room. "Jesus, it's good to see you," he said. "You look every bit as horrible as I had imagined." Her black eyes were beginning to rot into a ghastly green-yellow, and her left hand remained wrapped in bandages. He plunged straight into a narrative of all that he and seen from his cell.

"The guy who did the sticking was a hired killer, a known hit man who called himself the Garbage Collector. The other two were flotsam and jetsam, new to the pen, new to this state. Who put them up to it I don't know. It's hard to pick anything up during a lock-down. I've heard talk on the toilet phone that La Vida Loca might be involved, but Big Man vehemently denies it. He says he's a strong Union man."

"I know who hit me," said Teresa. She told him of her night in the hospital, and ended with her afternoon encounter at the information desk. "Raphael heard from him, and now thinks it was a mistake."

"Mistake, my ass. Are you sure it was the same man?"

"Positive. He had glasses on at night, but he was the same size, same color, same hard shape."

"Chino," the Fly said grimly, "is a very famous man. He founded La Vida Loca along with Big Man."

"Big Man?"

"That's the only name he goes by. Jose Ochoa is his real name—I only know it because I've been his lawyer. He's not really very big physically, but I'd bet a parole date on him against any two people in the world." The Fly's face screwed up in puzzlement. "Big Man is playing some kind of double game. I know him pretty well, I knew him in Folsom and I'm doing legal work for him here—him and one of his sidekicks. For someone in that line of business he's a right guy—I mean, he's consistent. Or he was . . ."

The Fly emerged from his reverie and looked directly at Teresa. "Anyway, I've made a decision. Fuck the Convict Code, I'm going to tell everything I saw. Do you have any problem with that?"

"Oh, no, none at all."

"Listen, is this information of yours patented?"

"Only where you got it. You can act like you learned it from thin air."

"All the better. No one believes you in here if you cite to a source. I'm going to do some spreading as well as sniffing. Will you still come and see me after I become a snitch?" Beneath the Fly's nonchalant grin was a trace of fear.

"Of course I will." Teresa remembered the first time they had met, how irascible and formidable he had seemed. She turned to the list of questions she had prepared for him to answer on the witness stand, questions she brought to Lagrimas just five days earlier to review with him. A stab of regret at the sight of her own large, eager handwriting blurred her vision.

"What's the matter, Teresa?"

"Oh, just everything that's gone wrong, that's all." She laughed helplessly, and was frightened at such an inappropriate noise coming from her mouth. "Let's go over these," she said, and they reviewed her questions. She questioned and cross-examined him; he performed superbly on both counts. The exercise restored her. She looked at the wiry little old man across from her and laughed again.

"What's up now?" the Fly demanded. He was worried.

"Oh, nothing. I'm just, how do they say it, emotionally labile today."

"Hey, that's bad, but its a helluva lot better than 'flat affect'! I've seen guys catch a life sentence because of their 'flat affect.' "

"Why don't you get out of here?" she blurted.

"What?"

"You heard me. It wouldn't be hard. If you wanted to, you could be out within a year."

He paused for a moment, and said deliberately, "Life is better for me in here than it ever could be outside."

"That's *non*sense, an affectation of yours. There's a whole world out there—"

"And a whole world in here. Outside or inside, both places are run by gangsters. One can adjust, make arrangements to live beneath or to the side of the big guys, but I know a helluva lot more about making a place for myself in here. It's a village, and I have a slot."

"But look around! You're in trouble now, aren't you, and it will be worse after you testify."

He shrugged. "It's a little tough, but it's been tough before. I can deal with whatever problems come up. People here are either glad I'm around, or they stay clear of me because they know how I will respond, and who my friends are. It's been that way for twenty years. I'm an asset because I have a useful skill. Sooner or later, they'll need me somewhere, and I'll go.

"Who the hell am I outside? Outside, I'm a defrocked teacher, an unlicensed bum with no chance of ever doing real legal work, the only thing I understand. Here I'm a good man to know, a potential key to the door. My skill earns me respect, some pocket change, and you know what? It even provides me sex every now and then with some young man desperate to get out, for whom it's a trivial thing, in a place where the desire of an old man for youth is laughed at but taken for granted instead of looked on as some kind of satanic horror. The US of A is a damned dangerous place for a little old faggot who lacks the money required to live in a part of town where the police and the punks will leave you alone."

The Fly was becoming quite agitated. He looked over his shoulder at the wall behind him. "Outside I would have my poverty rubbed in my face every day, every hour, and the cant, the hypocrisy—here—" the old man fumbled with his wallet, and produced a newspaper clipping—"check this out, President Gerald Ford, the amiable bumbler, a man no one describes as violence-prone or as a monster—speaking of the bombs he ordered dropped on the Cambodians one month after the North Vietnamese rolled into Saigon, because they grabbed one of our ships. He was ecstatic! All of our leaders, Democrats too, praised it as an act of 'stern resolve'! It turned out that we bombed our own people and shot down a helicopter with thirteen of our Marines—dozens of our people and hundreds of theirs died, and the Cambodians had already released our ship! Was it regarded as a fuck-up? Hell, no, exactly because it showed we were dangerous, a little crazy. The extra deaths *were a good thing*. It showed us 'taking initiative'; the fact that the whole mission was bullshit didn't matter as much as 'sending a message'. What's the real message? You're not tough enough unless you're willing to kill wild, to draw innocent blood.

"I keep clippings like this around so I don't lose perspective. What's the difference between the people who order this kind of act and the penitentiary 'gangs' of men sticking close to others of their own language, color, neighborhood, shifting alliances as needed to war against everyone else? Not a goddamn thing. I hear what its like out there on my radio—every ad a drumbeat for the Bicentennial. Patriotism is the last refuge of shoddy products. Now that I can order the books I want, why the hell should I get out of here? What's so fucking hot about the Free World?"

The old man's jaw set with his last words, and he stared over Teresa's shoulder into space. She was overwhelmed, and muttered, "Sorry I asked. I thought that freedom . . ."

"Freedom!" the old man snorted. "I'm free here, so long as I don't care about leaving. The Parole Board wants my soul, of course, every year they ask me to show remorse, preferably with tears. Every year they ask me to go see one of their hack camp-follower psychiatrists or psychologists who lacks the knowhow to sell his services to a higher bidder than the prison system, so I can gain *insight!*"

His voice dropped, and came through a demonic smile. "Every year I tell the Parole Board that they don't know their asses from hot rocks, they haven't the foggiest idea what 'release readiness' really means. Every year, the parole board denies my parole. We're all happy. They get to put a mouthy old man in his place. I get to stay here, unhassled by any stupid fucking 'release program' that would have me learn some miserably paying totally useless job, or go to church or go to therapy and be supervised by idiots. My body's needs are satisfied. My mind and soul are free. I'm ready now to *testify!*"

He laughed and laughed, until she wanted to slap him. "You've made your case," she said.

"I'll make our case in court, too. I'll smoke 'em on the stand. You just keep everything moving ahead and watch out for yourself, okay?"

"Okay."

They were silent for a moment. His inexplicable glee infected her, and, against her better judgment, she smiled again.

When their visit finished Teresa waited to be escorted to the Hole to see Fred Johnson. She walked with a lanky prison guard she had never seen before across the visiting room and through the steel door. Past two side hallways between visiting staff offices was another steel door that led to the prison's main corridor.

The traffic was very sparse; its absence allowed her to see that the corridor stretched towards infinity in both directions like the space of a dream, with no beginning or end. Her escort followed her, directing her from the rear, until they came to S-Wing. The two of them waited until another guard with a key appeared to let them into an anteroom. A guard peered through a small window, and when the door behind them to the main corridor was locked, he opened the door in front.

Though the journey was quicker than the trip to the Hole in Folsom, the same fear crackled in the air, a tension so violent it made the regular visiting room seem like a high school cafeteria with ash trays. After much whispered discussion among the guards, Teresa was told to wait in an empty staff office next to the central area. Two sides of the corner office were made of glass. She sat on display at a desk covered with Memoranda, Orders, Reminders and Directives, all littered with broken pencils, eraser grit, wadded carbon paper and twisted staples.

Eventually Fred was fetched by several guards. Teresa turned her head away as he was stripped of a yellow jumpsuit several sizes too big and searched. A moment later the office door was opened and Fred sat across from her. He looked very tired; his body moved as if it were not completely occupied, and his hollow eyes blinked as if he had just emerged from a cave. Five guards lingered in the room outside the glass.

"What the hell happened to you?" he asked.

Teresa remembered her face. "You first."

"I was headin' to see the Fly, somethin' about my case," Fred began. He talked for several minutes, becoming steadily more animated as Teresa took notes. "When they got to me I was in kind of a shock, kneeling by Serge. They whomped on me a while an' drug me into a strip cell. I been layin' up there ever since, waitin' for a murder beef. Only people come and see me is somebody pushin' food through a slot and a cop named Crescimani."

Teresa told him of her night in the hospital. She described the general appearance of the man who had struck her, and wrote his name on her legal pad. Fred stared at the name for a moment. "You know 'bout Big Man, the other dude?" he whispered.

"Yes."

"He sounded me out a while back about the Union. I didn't leave him any doubts on where I stood—but this whole bidness just don't seem like his *style*."

One week later Teresa received a letter at Joann Reilly's from the Fly, without a Lagrimas return address. "One of the many advantages of my exalted position as ruler of the law library," he wrote, "is the chance to meet people like the one who is mailing this letter for me. To the point: The Vida Loca will be moving to their own private wing at the end of the lockdown. They've been chasing that wing since February, when they first arrived here in force. I helped Big Man draft his administrative appeal to Sacramento after he was shot down by the warden. Now they've got it.

"I succeeded in sending Big Man all his legal papers, along with a message that he can find someone else to read and write for him. Its clear to me that the Warden bought the Vida Loca for a few pieces of silver and a private wing.

"What can we do? I plan on poisoning the well as much as possible in regard to all business dealings with the Vida Loca. Anyone who stands for the Union will swing their trade to another store. Who knows what that will mean, if anything? Unfortunately, I don't see any way to bring down on the head of the Warden the bucket of shit he deserves, but I'm thinking about it.

Yours in the Trenches,\
Z-1454"

23

Oliver Washington turned his new Toyota into the employees' parking lot at Lagrimas and muttered a quick prayer for the lifting of the lockdown. He was counting the days. After working ten straight, twelve hours a day, time-and-a-half overtime, double-time on the weekend, he was money ahead, but he would be very glad to cut back on his daily imprisonment.

"Washington!" he heard when he checked into B-Wing, his current assignment. "Take Gutierrez's file to Captain Crescimani's office."

"What's up?"

"Anybody who might be a Vida Loca member's going to Z-wing when the lockdown's lifted."

"No shit. What's that about?"

"Got me. Authorization sheet's on my desk."

Oliver went into Sergeant Walker's office and found a pink dittoed sheet of paper signed by Captain Crescimani asking for the files of thirty-odd men with Spanish surnames; Angel Gutierrez's name was in the middle, marked with a big red check. As he crossed the hall to the counsellor's office, two barred cell doors slammed and the heavy door to the wing closed with a jarring boom that froze him briefly in his tracks. Like working in the middle of a damned firing range.

ONE STEP AT A TIME. EASY DOES IT. TODAY IS THE FIRST DAY OF THE REST OF YOUR LIFE. The counsellor's office walls were papered with the same old dust-covered homilies. Oliver imagined a new crop while he sat and waited: IT TAKES ONE TO KNOW ONE. MONKEY SEE, MONKEY DO. NO MATTER WHERE YOU GO, THERE YOU ARE. ANGEL GUTIERREZ. Gutierrez had been very subdued around the wing since Oliver had seen him in Sanchez' office. A new wing with his buddies ought to pep him up.

The counsellor brought Oliver two files labelled *Central* and *Confidential* and a receipt to sign. Oliver fingered through them as the counsellor walked off down the hall. On an impulse, he searched for and found the Form CDC-1087 (PERSONAL INFORMATION). He looked at the top of the form to see where Angel had been born; the entry indicated *unknown (Mexico?)* Under the pertinent space—*Family Members*—he noted one entry: *Unknown or none.*

Crescimani was not in. Oliver gave the files to the secretary and walked slowly back down the long, deserted main corridor. When he reached B-Wing he hesitated, and then continued on to the visiting wing. The prison kept two 11" x 14" stiff cardboard sheets for every prisoner in Lagrimas, one at the Entrance Building and one in an office at the Visiting Wing. The name of every visitor and the date of every visit was inscribed on these sheets.

The records office was two doors down from Sanchez's corner office. After a moment's banter with the guard on duty, Oliver searched through the cards for *Gutierrez.* He found several. Some of the cards were well-thumbed, scribbled on with various pencils, ball-point and felt-tip pens. The card of his particular *Gutierrez,* Z-18127, was a spotless lined white, unblemished by even a single entry. No one, not even a lawyer, had ever come to see Angel Gutierrez during his four years of incarceration.

Oliver had read every word in the newspapers about the burst of F-Wing violence and its aftermath, and spent many hours conjecturing over coffee with fellow employees and the few prisoners with whom he could talk. The incident pained him, most directly because he regarded Fred Johnson as one of the best men in the prison. Magon's words to the Director busting the Warden for secretly shutting down the IAC were delivered before a large, appreciative audience. Few doubted the violence was aimed at the union the convicts were trying to start.

Oliver returned to his station. He reviewed everything he could of the events on the morning of July 3, frame by frame: Sanchez' face, Angel's tone and glances, his own surprise at seeing Angel alone on Sanchez' telephone.

"What's on your mind, honey?" his wife demanded one evening after three days of watching her husband brood. "Am I gonna get you back when they lift that lockdown?"

"You got me right now. It's prison, baby. Gimme a coupla more days and we'll talk about it." He reached for his wife, and stayed with her for hours. The following morning he broke the speed limit, and reported for duty without a moment to spare.

"Seen the paper yet?" Walker asked.

"Haven't even brushed my teeth. What's in it?"

Jennings pointed to his desk. GANG LEADER HOSPITAL ASSAILANT? shouted the headline. Attorney Teresa Suchil reported seeing a man with three teardrops tattooed under his left eye in the hospital on the afternoon before she was assaulted. The description corresponded to Enrique "Chino" Cantu, said by the paper to have a reputation as the founder of the prison gang La Vida Loca. Cantu was released to Grapevine on parole the previous March, and had apparently absconded from parole; his parole officer had not seen him for three weeks, and did not know where he was.

What would Crescimani say if Oliver told him about Angel using Sanchez' phone to call a family member that didn't exist? Oliver dialed the captain's office twice without success; the line was busy. Crescimani, with his pink face pinched into a permanent sniff, reminded Oliver of a chronically outraged rabbit. Why were Angel and all the rest of La Vida moved? It occurred to Oliver that Crescimani might already know about the call from Sanchez' office. He decided not to call just yet, and went through the motions of a day's work.

Oliver Washington had been very, very happy when he learned that the California Department of Corrections had hired him. The salary and benefits were far beyond the norm of the people who lived in his neighborhood on the wrong side of the highway that bisected Grapevine. He had notions that he could help people; he got along with all different kinds, and knew the pressures and circumstances that put men in prison. "What a fool I was," he muttered aloud, remembering his illusions as he drove home from prison after work. The heat was scorching, the hottest part of a July day at the time of year when hot weather was so relentless it felt eternal, and Grapevine became a dusty corner of hell.

He went to work with his father fixing cars the week after he graduated from junior college, but his whole family knew he was destined for better things. They celebrated his new position with a party. He even swung an assignment at Lagrimas, and after nine months made the day shift.

The problem with being a prison guard, thought Oliver, is that it is an empty job. In his Training Sessions he heard that he was to "avoid fraternization," that "our profession is on the front lines of law enforcement." And then it was over. All he had done since was fill in innumerable blanks(a task said by the old veterans to be a product of the "goddamned lawyers"), and wait. The clock inched along, slower than it had in junior high school.

The business with Angel and Sanchez had made the job worse than empty. He drove past orchards, suburbs, and junkyards without seeing, and slowed down as he reached his freeway exit. In the shop a man did real work—repairing broken things, getting people back on the road. At the very least, you can look back at the end of the day and see pieces of metal moved from one place to another, and know that you did something. He was starting to catch on when he left to be a prison guard, and hadn't learned anything real since.

In fact, Oliver had learned much—about procedure, record-keeping, accepting, delegating and dodging responsibility, all the lessons offered by a large organization to a cog whose eyes are open. He saw the trail ahead, but it did not beckon.

White guards viewed him with fear or contempt according to how they assessed his intelligence. He thought he could see them age before his very eyes, their bodies swell up, their hair grizzle, their skin wrinkle and blotch, just as he felt as a child that he could see the corn grow in the backyard as he sat still in the garden on warm July nights.

When his father's chief assistant had left the shop in the spring, he had talked to his dad about his unhappiness at Lagrimas. His father nodded slowly, and put in words what Oliver could see; the shop was doing fine, cars were everywhere, people were paying their bills. It was a good business. They had gotten along fine together ever since he moved out of the family house and into a place with Margaret nine blocks away. The money wasn't as certain as the check from the State, but the shop had been OK for over 15 years and was getting better—so what if he had to wash grease off his hands at night?

The vacant lot next door to the garage his father had purchased four years earlier was covered with dust. Even the thistles were now dead pillars of dirt.

"Hey, daddy," he called. "Four o'clock, time for a break."

"Oliver, how you doin'!"

"Oh, pretty good, I guess—how 'bout a cup of coffee, on me, eh?"

Two damaged radiators hissed and sputtered across the garage. Wendell Washington was about to beg off, but he saw his boy was exceptionally agitated. He talked to his mechanic, and walked with Oliver to the Eagle Cafe.

Oliver looked out from their booth through a plate glass window at heat waves rolling up from the street, and shivered involuntarily. His uniform was askew; buttons unbuttoned, tie loosened wide. Wendell could not recall seeing his son so disturbed in quite a while. It was not Oliver's style to make fusses for the thrill of it; he was more likely to swallow whatever was going on and wait it out. Wendell looked intently at Oliver, and felt a surge of love and concern. He turned away as his son shuffled uncomfortably under the weight of his gaze.

"What's up, son? You ain't lookin' so good. You havin' problems at work?"

Oliver sipped his coke, grateful for the direct question. Memories of how happy everyone had been when he took the Corrections job interfered like radio static with what he wanted to say.

"You still need help around the shop?"

"Sure I do. What happened, you run over the warden's foot?"

"Not yet, but I'm thinkin' about it. Remember that stabbin' that came down last week?" Oliver plunged in; he wanted to hear the whole story himself to see how it sounded. He told his father about Sergio Magon and Fred Johnson and the convict's union and what happened when the director came to visit, and what had happened on the morning of July 5 and how he had been sent to the front gate and Sanchez' office in the Visiting Wing to cancel attorney visits, and about Angel and the morning's story about Cantu and the Vida Loca, and the rules around phone calls and what he had felt when he saw Gutierrez alone on the phone and what Sanchez had said; and he told his father about La Vida getting a wing of its own, and what he had found out from Angel's file.

"Sanchez was lyin'," he concluded. "I can see that man in my mind's eye as clear as day. And there's nobody around there I can talk to. The bigwigs have turned around and given that gang everything it wanted."

Wendell stroked his chin, and shifted his position on the soft foam seat. "Sounds to me like the warden bought off that Vida bunch to do in the union—Sanchez 'll likely be promoted any day now."

Oliver heaved an immense sigh, feeling the relief of having dumped a heavy load of accumulated broodings. Right or wrong, at least he wasn't crazy.

"What's on your mind to do?" his dad asked.

"I'm gettin' out of that slime bucket." Oliver was surprised at his own vehemence.

"You're thinkin' 'bout kickin' it over as you go."

"Right."

"You aimin' to be a hero?"

"No, but—"

"I'm not gonna tell you to keep it to yourself. I *am* gonna remind you that you dealin' with some bad people. Seems to me the smart thing to do is to put it out in such a way that you either don't show up at all, or if you make any appearance on the stage, you be some dummy in the corner that everybody moves on past."

"What do you mean?"

"I want to think about it some. Come on to supper tonight, bring Margaret with you, and we'll all figure it out."

24

Lieutenant Sanchez spent the languid lockdown days considering who, if anyone, should learn of his role in Magon's stabbing. It was a villainous business, and he did not care for a public identity as the villain. On the other hand, the few who knew, Captain Crescimani and maybe two or three others in that clique, were treating him with undeniable respect. There were certain other staff members whom he would have know what he did. Especially the Warden.

Crescimani prepared an Order, signed by the Warden, to move all known Vida Loca members to their own Wing once the lockdown was lifted, on grounds of "protecting institutional security". When the local paper ran a story pointing a finger at Chino Cantu and the Vida Loca as involved in the hospital stabbing, Sanchez held his breath. But it was all working out for the best. The news left the impression that the violence was between two gangs fighting, the kind of thing prisons are famous for. Things were going so well that Sanchez leaned strongly toward letting several people know of his role; the chief question in his mind, as he idled away weeks with no visitors to manage, shifted from whether anyone should know to how they should be informed.

His mind drifted to this question one late July afternoon while he sat at his desk sketching with a pencil tentative rearrangements of the visiting room furniture. He had seen the Warden once in the aftermath of the stabbing. The Warden had nodded absently to him, preoccupied with other concerns. He couldn't very well walk up to the Warden and say, "Warden, I was the one who decapitated half the Union and fatally blemished its image. Me, the one who knows how to serve you effectively." It would be best if Crescimani dropped a solid hint on the Warden, something like, The Warden says, "Thank God the Union's out of my hair!", and Crescimani reflects quietly, looking off toward the corner of the Warden's office, "Sanchez is the one to thank." The Warden, sensing that he is on dangerous ground, doesn't probe further, but that night, as he prepares for bed, the Warden sighs gratefully as he buttons his pajamas and thinks that Sanchez really is the kind of man he needs as Program Administrator.

The ringing of the telephone jarred him loose from his reverie. "Sanchez, visiting," he answered.

"Lieutenant Sanchez? I'm Joann Reilly with the *Daily News*." He knew this call was coming. She had done all the stories for the local paper and had already interviewed several line officers and almost all the staff officers about gangs in prison. Everyone said the interviews were a piece of cake, questions about whether gang members had secret handshakes, that sort of thing. He had considered whether to cooperate, and decided that he would be much more conspicuous if he refused to see her. They agreed to meet after the day shift ended at Perko's Koffee Kup in the Figtree shopping center. She would wear a straw hat, and meet him at the door.

After he ordered coffee, she asked him if he knew anything about a gang called the Vida Loca.

"Yes, I've heard talk about such a group."

"As you may know, a man said to be one of their founders had been identified as the man who assaulted Sergio Magon and Teresa Suchil in Community Hospital. Do you have any idea why they worked so hard to get Mr. Magon?"

The reporter waited for his answer, her pen poised over a tiny red memo book. "No idea. I think probably it was some kind of hassle between two groups, the Union that Magon worked for and the other one, but as to why, I could only guess." He arched his eyebrows, looked over his shoulder, lowered his voice, and said confidentially, "Time and again, we find that drugs are at the bottom of these kind of problems."

She shared his concern with a nod, and asked, "How is it that gangs on the inside communicate with their members on the outside, especially when everyone is supposed to be locked in their cells?"

A little tricky, but Sanchez was ready. "Miss Reilly, the truth is, we're terribly understaffed. Lagrimas is a huge prison. How do they get drugs inside? How do they reach outside? Our prison is like a city. Its very large, and we just don't have the manpower to properly supervise every prisoner like we should." The lieutenant hoped his plea for more staff was quoted; if so, he would have to figure out some way to be sure that the Director saw the story. Perhaps he could simply mail it anonymously.

"Lieutenant, one of the members of the Vida Loca has stated that you asked him to kill Sergio Magon or some other member of the Union of the Imprisoned, and that you promised his gang a private wing in exchange."

Sanchez' cup and saucer rattled. He could barely believe his ears. "What did you say?" he sputtered.

"He has signed a confession naming you, and says you made the offer on behalf of the Warden. He says that he used your telephone to order the hospital assault."

The vinyl beneath him became slippery. His deodorant weakened and collapsed under a tidal wave of sweat; he could smell himself. "Miss Reilly, let me tell you something about prisoners." He pushed the words out, and was surprised at their normal tone. "Hell, prisoners will say anything to get a break. They'll lie, accuse their own brothers of whatever—"

"His name is Angel Gutierrez. He was seen talking to you in your office."

"I talk—I talk to dozens of inmates every day about one aspect or another of their visiting situation." She was looking straight at him, boring in like a godamned termite. He hadn't properly prepared. "Look," he said, in a voice turned icy, "What are you getting at? What the hell do you want?"

"Gutierrez was seen using your telephone just after Magon was stabbed. You told a fellow officer at the time that he was calling his family."

Fucking Washington. She must have interviewed every officer in Gutierrez' wing. "I often allow an inmate to use the phone if his situation has changed in regard to receiving a visit. It's a matter of convenience to his family. And anyway, I do not like being interrogated by an arrogant little—" he stopped himself. "If you'll excuse me, I. . ."

She reached into the file folder under her memo book. "I've obtained copies of Angel Gutierrez' files along with his statement. He has no family in the United States. He's never received a visit."

From a manila folder came two administrative appeals by Jose Ochoa on behalf of the Vida Loca asking for a private wing filed over the previous eight months that were turned down by the Warden, and a Movement Order signed a few days earlier by the Warden authorizing a separate wing for La Vida Loca. "The payoff has been made by the Warden, the only person in a position to make it."

The Warden. He was getting disoriented, and looked around; the restaurant was crowded with people, none of whom he knew.

"Miss Reilly, I'm not—"

"Lieutenant, wait. I want to help you. I believe you were forced into this ugly business. I've learned that the Warden has been embarrassed by Sergio Magon and the organization he represented. It's clear to me that the Warden put some kind of pressure on you to bear the burden of doing his dirty work."

"Hey, wait a minute." Her line of thinking was intolerable. "The Warden had nothing to do with any of it."

"Nice try, but he signed the Order. He's the one with a motive, and—"

"Look, don't print anything about the Warden. A lot of people don't like the Union, not just him. He only approves those orders, its Captain Crescimani who's in charge of movement. The Warden had absolutely nothing to do with it, he doesn't know anything." Sanchez swiftly played back all the reporter had said. Time for damage control. "This guy Angel came to me one day and said he would see that a Union leader got hurt if the Vida Loca could get their wing. I knew they were likely gonna get that wing anyway, we've done that with other gangs to get them out of the way. It keeps everything safer. I told him it would be wrong, but I didn't think much of it. I admit, I should maybe have done more, in light of what happened. He came by later and said he needed to make a phone call home about a visit. I said OK, make it quick, and left my office to take care of some business in the file room down the hall. I came back in two, three minutes—Washington can tell you, I wasn't there when he phoned."

"Did you talk to Captain Crescimani about any of this?"

"Hey, are you going to print anything tomorrow?"

"No, I'm not. I don't know enough yet."

The hell you don't, thought Sanchez. He got up to leave. "Well, don't print anything about the Warden. You haven't got a damned thing to link him up to something this awful. It would just be—be scandal-mongering, yellow journalism."

"Lieutenant, I don't print material that has not been verified."

Sanchez waited at the cash register to pay for his coffee. The reporter left her seat and walked past him and out of the restaurant. A striped red and green Mexican purse swung slowly by her side, as if it contained something heavy. He gave the cashier a dollar, and realized he had not seen the purse while they talked. Lieutenant Sanchez ran out of Perko's Koffee Kup without his change. He walked hurriedly up and down between the rows of parked cars, but she was gone.

The most soothing activity Lieutenant Sanchez knew of was watering his lawn, measuring out the miraculously fresh and unlimited water over his grass and flowers. July required special vigilance. Five times a week he watered by hand, uncoiling a green hose and using his thumb to vary the spray's width and distance. Usually he waited till sunset for maximum absorption, but after the encounter at Perko's he grabbed his hose in the high heat of the day at 5:00, and began to spray. The water jetted back and forth in lazy loops over the back and front yards, pausing to saturate the patches that seemed most thirsty.

His wife waved at him through their picture window as he watered; he waved back and thought, no fucking doubt about it, he was going to roll up Angel Gutierrez and send him to Protective Custody. All Angel's partners would consider him a cowardly snitch, and mark him for death. Gutierrez would fight it, but his public resistance would seem like an effort to cover his tracks. He might even get knocked around—hell, he *would* get knocked around—during the move. Sanchez could do it easily, make up an anonymous note imputed to Angel himself claiming death threats from an unspecified source, and then write the Order.

In the flowerbed on the house's south side, the pansies had already begun to droop badly, after only one day without water. The possibility that the reporter was lying about what Gutierrez had said did not escape him, but Sanchez could not remember Gutierrez ripping off his telephone without wincing. The little fucker had pushed him around, in his own office. It really didn't matter as far as Gutierrez was concerned if the reporter told the truth; Gutierrez had to go.

Gutierrez was moved near the end of July by five staff members, kicking and screaming all the way. Sanchez was gratified to hear that Angel had made deep toothmarks into Oliver Washington's thumb. Nothing appeared in the press. The lockdown ended on August 1; Sanchez's job became one frantic scramble all day long coping with the pent-up pressure of visitors.

Then, on August 3, the newspaper stories began. Lieutenant Sanchez had the paper delivered to his house each morning. Normally, a glow of satisfaction warmed him when he opened his front door at 6:30 a.m. and saw a freshly made, tightly bound paper on the porch. Sometimes it wouldn't be there; he would then, holding back his dismay with some difficulty, walk down the steps in his slippers and peer about under the bushes. The sigh of relief he exhaled upon spotting the paper hiding next to his drainpipe was so pleasurable it made the moment's tension preceding it a worthwhile investment. On those mercifully rare days when there was no paper to be found, Sanchez was so upset he did not regain his jovial demeanor until reaching the staff parking lot.

When the stories came, though, he lost all sense of morning anticipation. The first one appeared in the bottom left of the front page, and was entitled, PROFILES OF VIOLENCE. Sergio Magon was labeled as the "Victim", and portrayed as a bright young man led astray by drugs into petty crimes, none involving violence. His father, a senior field manager at the largest Thompson Seedless ranch in the county, was interviewed, along with two sisters. It was bad, slanted news—Magon's photograph was a charming civilian one, while the photos of the men who stabbed him were mug shots taken in prison. Their rap sheets were included; one had been convicted of murder for hire. The story included an eyewitness account that described three men jumping Magon and being beat off singlehanded by Fred Johnson; it concluded with a question: who hired the killers?

The next story focused on the Vida Loca and Chino Cantu. THE GROWING MENACE OF PRISON GANGS was the headline. The main story led off with HOSPITAL ATTACK SUSPECT BELIEVED

TO HAVE FLED TO MEXICO. Long interview with Teresa Suchil about the Union and its lawsuit, what Magon would have testified. Big deal about unsuccessful efforts to interview Big Man. Heavy implication that the Vida Loca was involved inside as well; question—what was the motive? The whole prison buzzed about it all day long.

The next morning, the lieutenant arose a bit later than usual, and decided to let the paper lie; there would be plenty of time to read it at the prison or when he returned home. He hastened through his preparations, and opened his front door to leave for work.

The paper lay before him, on the welcome mat. He stared at it, unable to move. Really, it was nothing but smashed tree pulp smeared with ink; but his legs refused to obey specific marching orders to get him on past and down the road. The telephone rang. With a sigh of relief he returned to the kitchen and answered. It was the Warden.

"Have you seen the paper yet?" the Warden demanded. He didn't sound in a good mood.

"No."

"Well, read it. Be here in my office this morning at eleven o'clock."

"Yes, sir!"

He moved mechanically back to the porch and picked up the paper. On page two, he found a story captioned LAGRIMAS GANG GRANTED PRIVATE WING. The Warden had been interviewed and was asked why he ordered the gang's movement after twice having refused it; the Warden was quoted as saying that he was only "considering" the move, in light of the recent violence, and cited news stories about Chino Cantu as a reason. But, according to a copy of the Movement Order obtained by the reporter, the Warden signed it on July 12, two days before the news story about Cantu broke. The Warden then put it off on Crescimani, who was "unavailable". The story ended by noting that all known Vida Loca members had been moved save one, who had been placed in Protective Custody.

Sanchez threw the paper down on his kitchen floor. Why the fuck doesn't she just come out with it? He was going to make the papers with the next story, sure as shit. He heard his wife stirring upstairs. It was after 7, past time to leave.

He had left his car in the driveway in front of the garage the night before. It seemed unnaturally low at first glance. Crossing his lawn to the driveway, he saw that the car had no wheels. All its windows were smashed. There were no longer any seats; the car's floor held only splintered glass.

He felt a chill penetrate his uniform. His eye travelled over the entire husk of his car. The hood was gone, as was the motor, the battery, and every other part that he could name save the antenna. A piece of paper impaled on the antenna contained a message written in Spanish: *Next time, Pubic Hair, go through the chain of command.*

He stood on his lawn for a long time. Finally he returned to his house, called the Warden's office and left a message that he would be late because of car trouble.

25

CAPTAIN CRESCIMANI APPEARED AT THE WARDEN'S OFFICE PROMPTLY at nine o'clock. He stood before the Warden's desk, which bore only a copy of the morning's issue of the Daily News, until the Warden pointed to a chair.

"What the hell is going on?" the Warden rasped. Crescimani waited for a more specific question, a temper tantrum, some kind of guidance; but none came.

"Nothing special," temporized Crescimani. "The Vida was moved because of a dangerous situation that has gotten more dangerous lately."

The Warden shook his head sadly. "I'm going to have to read every word of what you put on my desk from now on," he said, and Crescimani swallowed a lump that would not pass. The Warden had just told him he would soon lose his position.

"Oh, by the way," the Warden added, as if the thought had just occurred to him, "Do you happen to know why Magon was hit?" In spite of his effort to remain still, to create an atmosphere of mutual concern, Crescimani squirmed.

"Or," the Warden continued, with a distressing lack of hope in his voice, "who set Magon up? Why Gutierrez didn't go along to the wing with his buddies, or why Sanchez pulled him into P.C.? How can I function if I don't know what's going on in here? What are you worth if you don't keep me informed, Crescimani?"

"Sir, you should talk to Sanchez."

The Warden ignored him and leaned forward. He locked on to Crescimani and pinned the Captain back with the ferocity of his gaze. "Did you set up Magon?" the Warden whispered. "Was it you who got that twerp? Tell me, now."

It would be so easy to tell the Warden and so fatal, an easy death, like slipping down the gullet of a giant into quick oblivion. "No," he answered smoothly, "I did not."

"Well, who did? What have you heard? What has Sanchez said to you about it?"

It was very clear that he needed to give the Warden something. He paused, as if he were trying to recollect. His pause shifted gears and extended, to convey inner turmoil. "Sanchez did say something about it." He waited.

"Well, what was it, man? Tell me."

"He said that he was pissed about the Union. Hell, nothing special about that—but he complained that nobody was doing anything, and he said something like, If no one else is going to take care of business, he would. I thought—I still think—it was just a little loose talk."

"Sanchez. Why did you move Gutierrez?"

"I found a note on my desk saying he was going to get hit, signed by him."

"Why did he talk to you, instead of someone else?"

"I don't know."

"He says he never asked for it, that you rolled him up for no reason."

"What else can he say? He needs to hold up his head in public."

"Crescimani tells me he heard you talk about taking out someone involved with the Union, someone like Magon."

Crescimani had told the Warden. Sanchez paused to digest this fact.

"Did he also tell you that I talked to him first, and got his cooperation?" Sanchez asked. The Warden was silent. "I couldn't offer anyone a wing myself, you know. I'm nothing but a lieutenant." The Warden was impassive, inscrutable. "Someone had to do something!" Sanchez cried. "Everything was coming apart—"

"Everything was not coming apart. A few bumps in the road don't mean the road is going to end. Storms pass, Sanchez."

The Warden thought he was a fool. "Sir, the sight of you on the floor—"

"Goddammit!" roared the Warden, "That little pinch of misery was nothing compared to the shitstorm around me now!" He withdrew abruptly into a pensive, unfocused stare. "Everything points to me, Sanchez, not you. Don't you realize that? It was my signature on the Movement Order. People are talking about how Magon 'got' me in front of the Director. I'm looking like a savage, an animal—the kind of person who might murder a man because he embarrassed me."

A tear formed in the corner of the Warden's right eye, and fell as he turned toward Sanchez, twisting like a crystal knife through Sanchez's heart as it dropped. "I'm finished," said the Warden. "My career, the ideas I stood for, my hopes for the department—finished. I'm in a swamp of innuendoes and I'll never get out. "

"But—"

"Get out of my office," the Warden said quietly, and turned his back.

Sanchez walked briskly through the main corridor to his office. "Workin' hard?" sang out a fellow officer on his way to lunch.

"Hardly workin!" Sanchez replied as he strode even faster to the visiting wing. Half a minute in his chair was intolerable; he had to move. A few minutes later, he had signed out for the day and was wandering around the staff parking lot searching for his car, when he remembered that his car no longer existed. He stood still in the sea of vari-colored enameled steel vehicles. He had come in a rent-a-car, but could not remember exactly what it looked like.

The first thing he tried was to walk up and down every row, but nothing triggered any sense of recognition. Methodical effort. He pulled his keys from his pocket and began inserting them into each new mid-sized car. Since many of the vehicles were four-wheel drive jeeps, pick-up trucks, sport cars, or old clunkers, his task should not be too onerous. He looked up at the tower guard, and saw that the guard was looking down at him. He waved, and shrugged his shoulders as high as he could.

His twentieth try was successful. An immense thirst followed his rush of relief. Four miles down the highway, he pulled into a shopping center and turned into the parking lot of Perko's Koffee Kup.

He ordered iced tea and two glasses of lemonade. His head pulsed; he felt it expand and contract, expand and contract, as if something were straining to burst free. When the drinks finally arrived he was hanging on for dear life, squeezing the table so hard his knuckles were drained of blood. The slow-bouncing music at Perko's normally calmed Sanchez; now it was insistent. Everything around was pushing him on. He went to the phone booth, looked up the number of the Grapevine Daily News, and called, launching fervent prayers like mental darts in every direction that she be there.

"Joann Reilly, please."

"Whom shall I say is calling?"

"Lieutenant Victor Sanchez. Tell her it's urgent, it can't wait."

"I'll see if she's in."

Sanchez's prayers moved from his mind to his lips, and aimed toward his mother and the Virgin of Guadalupe.

"Lieutenant Sanchez?" Her voice was a cool, deep draught of what he needed.

"Yes. Miss Reilly. I have something important to tell you. I'm sure you'll be interested. I'm at Perko's Koffee Kup again. I need to see you. Right now."

After the phone call he stepped lightly into the rest room. The relief that coursed through his body banished any doubt that he was doing the right thing. He removed his uniform shirt and undershirt, and washed himself thoroughly, ignoring what might have been leers or sniggers from the other patrons. He would tell all, all, but he would stick it to the Vida Loca, pin it on the whole godamned gang, and stop the buck cold, right at himself—and Crescimani. Sweat stains had left faint loops beneath his arms, but overall, he looked sharp.

Miss Reilly was two minutes early. She sat down in the booth across and greeted him. For a moment he studied her features: thin lips, high cheekbones, narrow nose, dark, somewhat hollow eyes, feathery dark hair. God bless her, she didn't push. He began to talk; after a couple of minutes she asked him if she could record what he was saying. Oh yes, he answered, and felt lighter and more buoyant than ever as his moorings snapped one by one and the mainland fell away.

26

"Finally, Your Honor, violence in prison has always taken place in corners and shadows, and not at open meetings. The State has presented its own witnesses and intensively cross-examined ours, but its opposition remains no more than a generalized anxiety. I suggest that their real fear is of restraints being placed on their absolute discretion to do whatever they please inside the walls. They fear the intrusion of laws into a bastion of lawlessness where the kept have violated the law and the keepers resent being subject to any law at all.

"I believe the Constitution requires us to chop away at the arbitrary and capricious side of social life whenever the opportunity presents itself. You now have that chance. Thank you."

Teresa's closing rebuttal was finished. She sat down at the counsel table.

"Submitted?" asked the Judge.

"Submitted," said each attorney. Judge Pedrocelli thanked them for timely and thorough presentations, and indicated that he would deliver his decision from the bench after a twenty-minute recess. Teresa's stomach fell. She knew that if the judge intended to rule in their favor, or entertained any doubts about how to rule, he would take several days to draft an opinion.

When the bailiff called the court to order, all became quiet. The Judge praised the Union of the Imprisoned for its well-considered and imaginative approach to the intractable problems of prison administration. However, he held that the ultimate authority for prison administration, absent clear evidence of flagrant abuse, rested with the Director of Corrections, and that no such abuse was shown by the petitioners, only a plausible alternative. The petition was therefore denied.

"I'm constrained to add," continued the Judge, "that an element of my decision certainly was the recent outbreak of violence in Lagrimas. I don't mean for a moment that the violence was in any way instigated by the Union. The truth seems to run the other way; for whatever reason, a man scheduled to be a witness for the Union was attacked and killed. Its a fact of life, though, that new and controversial ideas can be like sparks in the tinderbox environment of a state prison. Ms. Suchil?"

Teresa stood, her face flushed with anger. "Your Honor, it not only is unfair to penalize the Union because it was assaulted, it's against the law. The U.S. Supreme Court has ruled that whoever voices an idea protected by the Constitution may not be punished because they were subject to a violent attack by others—"

"Ms. Suchil, I've made my ruling. If you don't like it, talk to the Supreme Court. Petition denied." As the gavel struck the bailiff told all to rise. Judge Pedrocelli disappeared, and the courtroom erupted into a babble of voices.

Over the five-day hearing, Teresa had adapted to a rhythm of frenzied preparation sandwiched around the slow ceremonious pace of performance in a court that sat in session six hours a day. She was dazed by the hearing's abrupt end and the tumult that followed. We were never likely to win, she told herself—think how much trouble it would have been if we had! But while still in the aura of the Judge's pronouncement she was crushed by the defeat, and passively accepted congratulations and consolations as she loaded up two briefcases with papers.

"Terry, you were great. You made our case. So what if we lose the silly goddamn lawsuit?" Union members had gathered for dinner in a Mexican restaurant before the long drive home.

"You sure have changed your tune."

"I know." Art swept up the remains of a dish of guacamole into his mouth. "I agitated long and hard to get this very lawsuit down the road.

The legal bug took a big bite out of my ass, no doubt about it. But I've always been a dumb son of a bitch. You know the way it works? The people who win lawsuits aren't people—you gotta be *immortal*, like the Department of Corrections or a corporation—or have the money to hire an immortal law firm. We've got speed and flexibility, but they've got forever."

"Take a look at labor," interjected Tyrone. "The workin' man lost every lawsuit he filed for years and years—judges turned him into a criminal if he didn't work in hellholes for shit wages, 'til the workers fought and died and got enough power together for some judge to discover they had a Constitutional right to organize. Why the hell couldn't no judge see in 1890 what they all saw in 1940? The *Constitution* hadn't changed. You can't expect nothin' outa these mothahfuckahs 'til you already got it."

"You all are such philosophers."

"We have to be, Terry," said Myrna quietly. "We're gonna keep going."

"Till the walls come tumblin' down." Art's blue eyes sparkled. Teresa searched his face for resignation or ambivalence, but found none. You could say he thrived on adversity, or you could say he was born to lose. . . .

She talked a moment about her plans to live with her children and set up a law practice in Oakland. Everyone listened attentively, and Teresa felt more alone than she had in years. "I'm doing the appeal," she said brightly, and everyone marveled as if they had spotted a pearl buried in their stack of tortillas. Her eyes glistened; she looked about blindly, and her left hand leapt across the table of its own accord to touch a startled Robert on his shoulder.

Angel Gutierrez had succeeded in combining the full weight of both the State and the Vida Loca against him. The prompt transfer of thirty-five members of the Vida Loca to their own Wing was very popular; if Big Man held any resentment, he kept it to himself. The newspaper story identifying Chino as the hospital assailant made Angel uneasy. Then, the police came to take him away to Protective Custody. He had heard nothing of any confession he purportedly made, and was confused and terrified. He fought and scratched like a man with nothing to lose, and absorbed a terrible beating. While in PC he heard that the transfer was cancelled, and that Vida members were being returned to where they had lived before. Rumors flew constantly, but real information was impossible to come by, until his counsellor told him he was going to the Hole.

Big Man and four others from the Vida Loca were sent to the Hole on the same day. That night, Big Man told Angel that he was going to die tomorrow. The next morning, all cell doors were opened, ostensibly for release to the exercise yard. The five Vida members walked over to Angel's cell, and stared him down until he began to whimper and cry. They watched him for another ten minutes before killing him. Angel's death was as light as a feather; no charges were ever laid, no investigation ever made.

27

"ROLL 'EM UP, FLY, YOU'RE ON A BUS OUTTA HERE TOMORROW MORNING."

"Bullshit. My parole hearing is here, next week."

"Here's the Order. You can walk or we'll carry you, don't matter none to me."

He scrambled frantically about distributing legal papers to clients along with barrages of advice that no one understood. Then, he sold what was marketable, and gave the rest away. He spent the night sitting on his bunk, waiting. Handcuffed, he climbed on a gray schoolbus with barred windows at 5:00 a.m., and rode into the blackness away from Lagrimas.

The bus avoided freeways and criss-crossed the valley's grid of secondary roads until it reached the foothills. As the day broke, the bus began snaking higher and higher. No one knew where they were going.

All day long they looped back and forth through the foothills. As rocky slopes and the gray exoskeletons of last year's grass gave way to a dense conifer forest, the sun went down and the cold began to bite. Hours later, the bus pulled into the Modoc Correctional Camp. After what seemed no more than a few minutes of sleep, the Fly was back on a bus.

He rode south the next day in the shade of the high wall of the Sierra's east side, and landed that night somewhere in the desert. The next day he bounced further south down close to the border where he spent a feverish night in a dormitory surrounded by Spanish murmurings and cries that never seemed to stop.

During the first few days of his bus riding, the Fly peered intently between the slats that covered most of his window, drinking in the scenery, but as sore bones, sleeplessness and hunger overcame him he lost interest in the world's details. He dozed intermittently, and feigned sleep to avoid company. His automatic pilot took what little control there was to take. The days and nights blurred into one unbroken ride as he finally succeeded in withdrawing from all sensations and impressions.

Two weeks passed without a letter from the Fly telling where he had been sent. Teresa called Lagrimas, and tracked him through three transfers as far as the California Conservation Center in Susanville. The trail ran out when a personnel sergeant insisted that no one by the Fly's number had ever been assigned there. According to Personnel Location in Sacramento, the Fly was still at Lagrimas.

Teresa methodically called each of the thirteen California prisons. When that failed, she called all of California's county jails, and tracked down the phone numbers of all the dozens of prison camps. She set aside a day to find him, but it wasn't enough, nor was a second day spent on the phone. The phone grew hot and slippery in each of her hands; she found a washrag and continued calling, rattling off her spiel like a telemarketer making cold calls on behalf of Universal Insurance: "Hello, I'm Teresa Suchil, attorney for inmate # Z-1454. . . . Thank you." She spent hours on hold, and frequently lost connection, but she persevered with a routine so formulaic that when a voice informed her that Z-1454 had just arrived she said "Thank you" and began to hang up the phone before the words penetrated.

"Oh! Where are you?"

"Huh?"

"I mean, which prison?"

"We're at Samuel P. Yount Corrections Camp, honey."

He was in a redwood forest just under the Oregon border, in the heart of wetness.

She left very early next morning and drove north. After nine hours of driving the air was so saturated that she could see nothing other than a blurred strip of road ahead bordered by huge tree trunks that disappeared into low clouds. Road signs and traffic jumped at her with no warning. Finally, she saw a small wooden sign with faded gold letters that marked the camp. A gravel road twisted over ruts, drainage ditches, and two live streams. Water dripped from above, oozed from below, and ran in all directions; the earth had absorbed all that it could hold. She bumped to a halt at a complex of bunk houses, shops for tools and machines, and an administration building.

The guard who checked her Bar card and the appointment sheet retreated to an office down the hall. They met in a wood-paneled waiting room heated by a wood-burning stove. No one else was around.

"You were hard to find," she said.

"I've been on the road."

He didn't look at all like she remembered, like the image she kept before her during her phone calls. His color had changed from mottled pink to the moist bluegray of dead fish. He seemed both shriveled and damp, like a dishrag indifferently wrung out. Nevertheless, she plunged ahead with what she had come to say.

"I want to offer you a job."

"What?"

"A job." She told him about her plans to open a law office in Oakland.

"But I'm still in prison. Haven't you noticed?"

"Its time you did something to get out," she said firmly. "Even if you don't want the job, the offer will help you get a parole date. I remember very well your fine reasons for wanting to be in prison, but just in case you want to change your mind, I would love to have a keen thinker and organizer like you in my office."

He fidgeted for a moment with a pouch of tobacco, and laboriously rolled himself a cigarette.

The Fly's color had returned. "You want to be forgiven," he said.

"What do you mean?"

"I'll be glad to set you straight, no job offer required. Let me tell you what would have happened to Magon had he lived." Teresa sat very still.

"You gotta remember, Magon was a junkie before he came to the pen. Well, he'd have a spectacular Welcome Home party, and his choice of two or three lousy jobs when he gets out. He might go to school, but it really wouldn't matter much, because the daily grind would be too flat for him, he would get back to the thing that has always drawn him the most. He'd chippy around, and pretty soon, he'd be strung out, swallowed whole by junk. Wouldn't be too long before he starts passing bad checks all over town on the strength of his family's reputation. Then, he'd steal his momma's tv set like he did the last time he was out and about, and the time before that. After he hocked everything in sight he'd run off to a big city slum, probably New York this time, he always wanted to see New York, and either die or get turned out by the cops as bait for someone bigger, or maybe get popped again if he were lucky and sent off to Attica, leaving a ton of sad anger and confusion back here in the valley.

"But! What's happening now? His mother burns a candle to him every night. Magon didn't sneak off in disgrace; he died trying to bring light into a world of darkness. He's a hero, a man brought down by murdering scum rather than by his own weakness. His family's last memories of Magon are of his warm and witty self in the visiting room, of his picture in the newspaper. Mexicans love martyrs even more than they love sugar; most all their national heroes were betrayed and murdered. A person's death shines back over their whole life, you know, and Magon left the kind of legacy money can't buy. He's a lucky man."

"A cynical motherfucker, aren't you?"

The Fly became dreamy as his eyes turned inward; he suddenly looked at Teresa. "Where's Chino?"

"I don't know."

"Don't you care?"

"Not really. Raphael told me it was a mistake, and—"

"A mistake! Magon is dead—"

"According to you, we should give Chino a medal for killing him—"

"And your nose is still bent. You don't care if he skates free, eh?" A sneer had crept into his voice.

Teresa became very composed. "Revenge for me is like golf or astrology, something I've never seen the point of."

"How about justice? Does that escape you too?"

"What would you have me do about Chino? Call the cops every day? Breathe hard and demand that the big strong men of the Union drop whatever else they're doing to run around looking for him? Do you want me to try to stab him or shoot him myself, or hire somebody I don't know with money I don't have and then wait around for reports on who hurt who? I don't have time to get stuck on it. My children will be with me again, and I am not free like you. They need to be fed three times a day, every day, and no magic hand comes out of the sky to put food on our table."

"Why did you take them back?"

"I miss them. Besides, the pressure on me to raise them is intense. Any man who abandons everything for his work is greatly admired; if his wife and children suffer or do without, that's unfortunate, like a tornado is unfortunate. But a woman who insists that the father of a child provide for that child while she throws herself into work is trashed and reviled as a heartless robot. And they really want to be with me now."

Teresa settled her gaze on him. The gold flecks around her pupils glowed softly. "I could use your help," she said. "I'm suing Lagrimas for Sergio's family, and you know far more about civil rights suits than I do, or anyone I know." She smiled. "It's not so bad out there. You won't be *free* anymore, of course, but there are wonderful things to see and do that cost very little or nothing at all. Robert Chime will be working with me, a beautiful young man, you remember him, don't you?" Their eyes met in an instant of lustful recognition.

"What's happening in Lagrimas?" he asked.

"Fred's looking good, they still haven't filed charges on him. Sanchez pled last week to being insane. He's facing conspiracy charges. The Warden looks clear, Crescimani is still up in the air. They're accusing each other now. I'm going to sue them all, and let God sort them out."

"A regular Simonette le Monfort, aren't you?"

"I need your help, Nathan." The sound of his given name reverberated through him for the first time in ages. "You're a good typist, a great filer, a top researcher and organizer, and you'll come cheap because no one else will have you. I'm not just begging for absolution when I offer you a job. But so what if I feel guilty? Is it such a bad thing to try and make reparations? What's wrong with that?"

He was silent for a moment, appraising her. "You're pretty fucking slick, Teresa," he finally said. "But this is crazy. The state still has my balls in a vault."

"They're sick of you in here, and would like nothing better than to toss you out. If you would just refrain from insulting the parole board one time, you'd be out on the streets in a minute. The food is *so* much better outside, Nathan. I can see you as a gourmet cook with a fastidious little kitchen, spices all neatly ordered, and a pot belly that children rub for good luck—"

"Stop it, please, stop."

"I'm sorry. This is all new to you, but I've been thinking about it for weeks. Look, here is a formal offer on my new stationery, and here I've written down all the details I could think of, where you could live, salary, what you would do. Think about it, and write me a letter."

A couple of guards arrived, and more began to leave.

Day shift was over. The Fly read intently what she had given him.

"Robert has discovered that he can become a lawyer in California without going to school if he's supervised by someone and he passes the Bar exam, so he plans on doing it, just like Abraham Lincoln."

"You and he are lovers, eh?"

"That's right." He continued reading. "It's a doomed affair, though. In a few years he's going to fall for my daughter in spite of all my best efforts, and I'll probably shoot them both. It's going to be very exciting, Nathan."

A staff member who had arrived for the swing shift told the Fly that he had better hurry to catch dinner. He nodded, and continued to read.

"So you're really gonna sue Lagrimas, eh?"

"Right."

"Isn't that like getting revenge?"

"It's more like cleaning up a mess."

His head remained buried in the papers she had given him. The job was out of the question, but she would not leave until she got a favorable response.

"You're missing dinner," she said.

"No. I'm saving room for all the fettucini out there."

She covered his right hand with both of her own.

"Take it easy," he said. "Before I come out of here I want the deal spelled out. No paper is filed without me looking at it. I organize the office. No hippy-dippy scattering of papers everywhere. A place for everything, and everything in its place. And, I want a percentage of the take."

"Yeah?"

"Yeah. An equity interest is what the nice people call it. If you can talk five days a week like you've been talking to me, we're gonna make a whole lotta money."

As Teresa drove away, the Fly returned to his dormitory, composing a letter of regretful reconsideration in his head. He had always known she was *socially* sassy, but had never seen her be *personally* sassy. . . . The bunks, which he had mercifully never noticed before, were crowded close together, and sagged badly. The wooden walls oozed, and buckets caught part of the water that never stopped leaking through the roof. His legal materials, books, and files had not yet found him, might never find him.

The Fly lay on his bunk, and tried to figure her out. The longer a formula eluded him, the more pleased he became. Were he to dream up a dream employer, it would not be her, but then, who else was asking? Of course he couldn't do it, he would have to be remorseful before swine to get out. It really wouldn't work.

The Fly had not emerged from his cocoon long enough to plan. Now, as he planned, his drawing board was blank. Teresa's offer hogged the space. He became annoyed at her, and then purchased some peace of mind by promising himself that he would at least carefully consider her offer.

The bell sounded that marked the last call for dinner. His stomach growled; he was ravenous. Pep in my step, he noticed as he moved quickly toward the chow line. His stomach was definitely rumbling. It was time to eat.

Epilogue
—July 4, 1976

Sergio lay still beneath the grape leaves in the hot afternoon. Crows circled above the vineyard and called his name, again and again. The sound of their calls penetrated through his skin and pulled him up from the fine dust of the thoroughly ploughed land and into the sky. He flew with them above the workers' quarters, the big shaded home of the patron, *the barns, roads, the fruiting trees and vines and the tiny figures who shaped them. They flew together up the river to the mountains, above the snow and ice and jagged rock peaks toward the sun.*

As the elevator carrying his body descended, the thin air chilled him. His heart then surged, and pulled him away from all he knew. He became nothing but the wrapping of his heart, and soared straight back toward the warmth and bright rushing light from which he had been created.

Single copies of *DOWN IN THE VALLEY*
may be ordered from:

Clear Glass Publications
1752 S.E. Hawthorne Blvd.
Portland, Oregon 97214

■

Bulk orders may be purchased from:

BOOKPEOPLE
7900 Edgewater Dr.
Oakland, California 94621
1-800-999-4650

*Type is set in Caslon
by Anna Taylor of Navarro, California*

■

*Cover design and illustration
by Vicki Trego Hill of El Paso, Texas*

■

*Printed on acid-free paper
by McNaughton & Gunn, Inc.,
of Saline, Michigan.*

■